Channel Tunnel
Trains

Channel Tunnel Trains

Channel Tunnel Rolling Stock and the Eurotunnel System

Peter Semmens
MA, CChem, FRCS, MBCS, MCIT, FRSA
and
Yves Machefert-Tassin
CEng, FIMechE

◄Folkestone Terminal, October 1993

Copyright © Eurotunnel 1994

First published in 1994 by The Channel Tunnel Group Limited,
Eurotunnel Exhibition Centre, St Martin's Plain, Folkestone, Kent CT19 4QD;
telephone 0303-270111

Code E440

ISBN 1 872009 33 6

The moral rights of the authors have been asserted.

A CIP catalogue for this book is available from the British Library.

The authors and Eurotunnel have made every effort to ensure the accuracy of the information contained in this book, for which Eurotunnel takes responsibility.
However, the Channel Tunnel and its rolling stock are an evolving system, and operating conditions may result
in changes to the procedures and equipment described in this book.

Diagrams: There is no common scale for the diagrams of locomotives and rolling stock reproduced in this book.
For the benefit of modellers and others, some vital dimensions are given in millimetres. A consistent scale has been used within each diagram
that contains these dimensions, so that other dimensions can be scaled from those given.

Cover photographs:
Front: Freight shuttle at the Calais Terminal
Back top: Unloading a freight shuttle at the Calais Terminal
Back centre: The freight and passenger-vehicle facilities at the western end of the Folkestone Terminal
Back bottom: Loading a passenger-vehicle shuttle at the Calais Terminal

Printed in Britain by Eyre and Spottiswoode Limited

Contents

Shuttle locomotive in the Tunnel

Channel Tunnel Trains tells the story of the design and operation of some of the largest, longest and most advanced trains in the world – and probably the most expensive as well. The challenge of producing complex, reliable, low-maintenance rolling stock extends beyond issues of design and construction. The operation of these trains is integrally linked with the Tunnel itself, its signalling and power systems, emergency and communication procedures. The international passenger and freight through trains that will use the Tunnel as well also form an important part of the equation.

Thanks must first go to Yves Machefert-Tassin, Eurotunnel's Adviser on Railway Engineering, and to Peter Semmens, who over many months have struggled to keep abreast with a fast-developing railway, and have taken immense pains to provide lucid explanations of often very complex systems. I am also most grateful to my many Eurotunnel colleagues who spared valuable time from the critical task of commissioning and testing the shuttles to help their research and check portions of the text.

This book will be read by everyone interested in understanding how these unique trains are built and operate, and how safety considerations are integrated into all parts of the design and operations procedure. It is published in both English and French, and provides many examples of how the Channel Tunnel system has helped to link British and continental railway design and practice and will perhaps hasten the creation of pan-European railway standards.

Alain Bertrand
Chief Operating Officer, Eurotunnel

7

The Channel Tunnel is designed to carry passengers and freight between Britain and continental Europe. The system that opened in 1994 – under the service name Le Shuttle – provides a no-booking on-demand service for cars, motor-cycles and lorries (and, from autumn 1994, coaches as well). Half the Tunnel's capacity is allocated to shuttle traffic, which consists of specially designed and constructed trains running between purpose-built terminals at each end of the Tunnel. Under a usage agreement signed between Eurotunnel and 'the Railways' (in this case British Rail and SNCF), the other half is allocated to passenger and freight through-trains that connect major British and continental destinations via the Tunnel. Both shuttles and through-trains operate on standard-gauge rail tracks.

The Channel Tunnel consists of three separate tunnels, each 50km long: two rail tunnels, one for traffic in each direction, and a central service tunnel. The tunnels were bored largely through chalk marl at an average depth of 45m below the sea bed (75m at the deepest point), and are lined with reinforced concrete or cast iron.

Eurotunnel's shuttles are extremely large in cross-section to enable them to carry different types of road vehicle. Passenger-vehicle shuttles carry cars and motor-cycles in double-deck wagons; single-deck wagons are used by road coaches, high cars and light vans. The

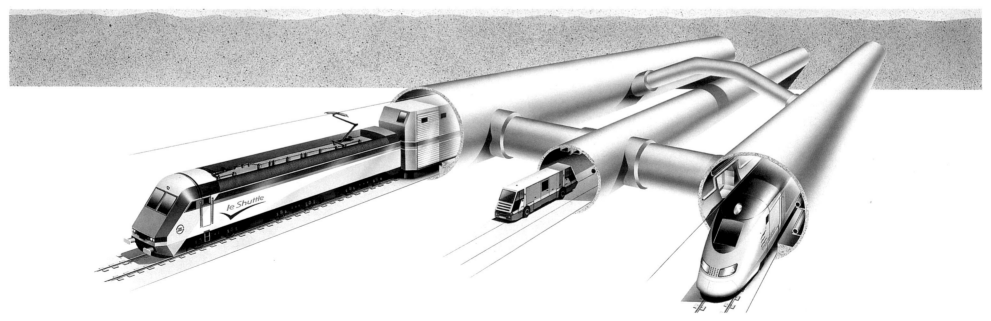

The three-tunnel system: trains travelling to France use the northern rail tunnel (left), those to the UK the southern rail tunnel (right). The smaller central service tunnel is used chiefly for maintenance purposes

separate freight shuttles carry lorries and their trailers weighing up to 44 tonnes.

The through-trains are run by other operators, including BR and SNCF. There are two types of passenger trains. Eurostar day trains are similar to the French TGVs, and are capable of speeds of 300km/h on suitable track. Overnight trains, which will include sleeping-cars, are to be introduced in 1995. Freight through-trains convey non-hazardous loads on any suitable wagon, many in containers or swap-bodies that are transferred to and from road vehicles at each end of their journey in special terminals throughout the European railway system.

The signalling system in the tunnels is designed to provide very close headways between trains in each direction. To make best use of this capacity, the shuttles must leave and arrive at the terminals in quick succession, where they have to be loaded and unloaded before their next journey. On emerging from the Tunnel, shuttles travel round a turning loop in each terminal before coming to a halt at long platforms, from which they then depart straight into the Tunnel. This reduces operating times and enables the shuttles to face in the right direction for departure.

Normally a shuttle never reverses its direction of travel. It traverses the turning loop in Britain clockwise, but goes anti-clockwise round the one in France, thus preventing uneven wear on the wheels. To achieve this, the departure track at the Calais terminal crosses the arrival track on a fly-over before entering the Tunnel. The system is thus shaped like a figure of eight, with two different-sized lobes.

For most of its length, the Tunnel system consists of two 7.6m diameter single-track rail tunnels, generally running parallel and 30m apart. Between them is the 4.8m diameter service tunnel. Cross-passages connect all three tunnels at intervals of 375m. These form part of the ventilation system, and also provide access to the rail tunnels for maintenance and emergency purposes. Every 250m piston relief ducts connect the rail tunnels. These ducts are designed to allow air to move into and out of the other rail tunnel, thus reducing the aerodynamic resistance of the trains passing through at speeds of up to 160km/h.

At two points underneath the Channel, the tracks in the two rail tunnels come together in a large crossover chamber, so called because linking crossover tracks have been built. In normal operation large steel doors separate the main tracks. The doors are retracted and the crossover tracks used whenever a section of one tunnel has to be temporarily closed for maintenance. When this

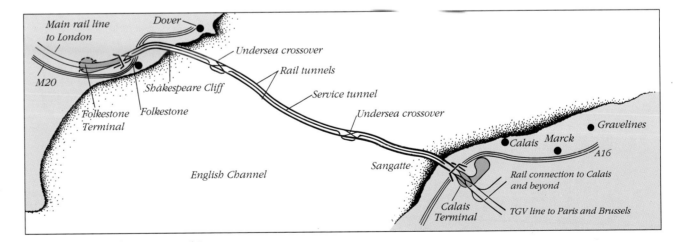

The Channel Tunnel in Britain and France

The approach to the toll booths at the entry to the Calais Terminal

Customs controls on the UK Terminal. Travellers clear both national customs, French and British, at the point of departure

The passenger terminal building at Folkestone, which contains shops and eating-places

Allocation lanes on the Folkestone Terminal, where travellers wait to board their shuttle

happens, single-track working operates in a section of the other tunnel. To enable the rail tunnels to approach each other, the alignment of the service tunnel drops below and to one side of the rail tunnels. Near each terminal the service tunnel also moves to one side, to allow road access to it without crossing the rail tracks. Two further crossovers are located near each terminal, just inside the portal on the British side, just outside it in France.

Fans on each side of the Channel ventilate the tunnels. The fans force air down the coastal shafts into the service tunnel, which is always maintained at a higher pressure than the rail tunnels. The air is distributed throughout the Tunnel system by means of controlled openings in some cross-passage doors; the passage of trains along the tunnels also aids circulation.

Eurotunnel has total control of the operation of the Tunnel system, including the terminals and tunnels themselves. This responsibility includes the signalling system, power supply, ventilation and drainage, as well as the road traffic in the terminals. It also includes the complete technical safety and security of all activities within these areas to ensure that passengers experience the easiest and safest journey possible.

To achieve this, many different designs and practices were studied, and compared with the arduous conditions likely to occur in operation in the tunnel system. Eurotunnel also enjoyed the unusual opportunity, and challenge, of designing the system from scratch. This made it possible to incorporate many new and complex features, even though it was recognised from the start that proven systems and designs were essential in order to minimise costly failures and delays during initial operations.

All trains that pass through the Tunnel – the passenger and freight through-trains as well as Eurotunnel's own shuttles – must thus comply with Eurotunnel's safety and operational standards. These in turn had to be submitted to the Safety Authority of the Intergovernmental Commission (IGC) before Eurotunnel was permitted to carry fare-paying passengers. The IGC was set up under the Treaty of Canterbury, signed by President Mitterrand of France and Prime Minister Margaret Thatcher of the UK on 12 February 1986, which marked the start of Channel Tunnel legislation in each country. The legislative process lasted rather more than a year; the French President signified his approval on 15 June 1987, and in the UK the Channel Tunnel Bill received the Royal Assent on 23 July. One month after the Treaty was signed, the two governments awarded the private-sector Eurotunnel Group a 55-year concession (subsequently extended to 65 years) to develop, finance, construct and operate the Channel Tunnel system; this also specified that no additional concession would be awarded to any other company before the end of the year 2020.

Eurotunnel consists of two separate companies, one based in Britain (Eurotunnel plc), the other in France (Eurotunnel SA). To finance the construction of the largest civil engineering project in Europe, the Company raised, by the end of 1993, some £9 billion. Approximately three-quarters of this was in loans from a syndicate of more than 200 banks throughout the world, led by four Agent Banks, Midland and National Westminster in Britain and Banque Nationale de Paris and Credit Lyonnais in France. Just under 20 per cent was raised from public share issues, and there were also significant loans from the European Iron & Steel Community and the European Investment Bank.

The contract to build and equip the tunnels and terminals, as well as to provide the rolling-stock, was awarded by Eurotunnel to a consortium of ten companies, operating as Transmanche-Link (TML). Transmanche Construction GIE carried out the work in France, and Translink JV on the British side.

Sunset over the toll booths at the Folkestone Terminal

Part One

Rolling Stock Design and Equipment

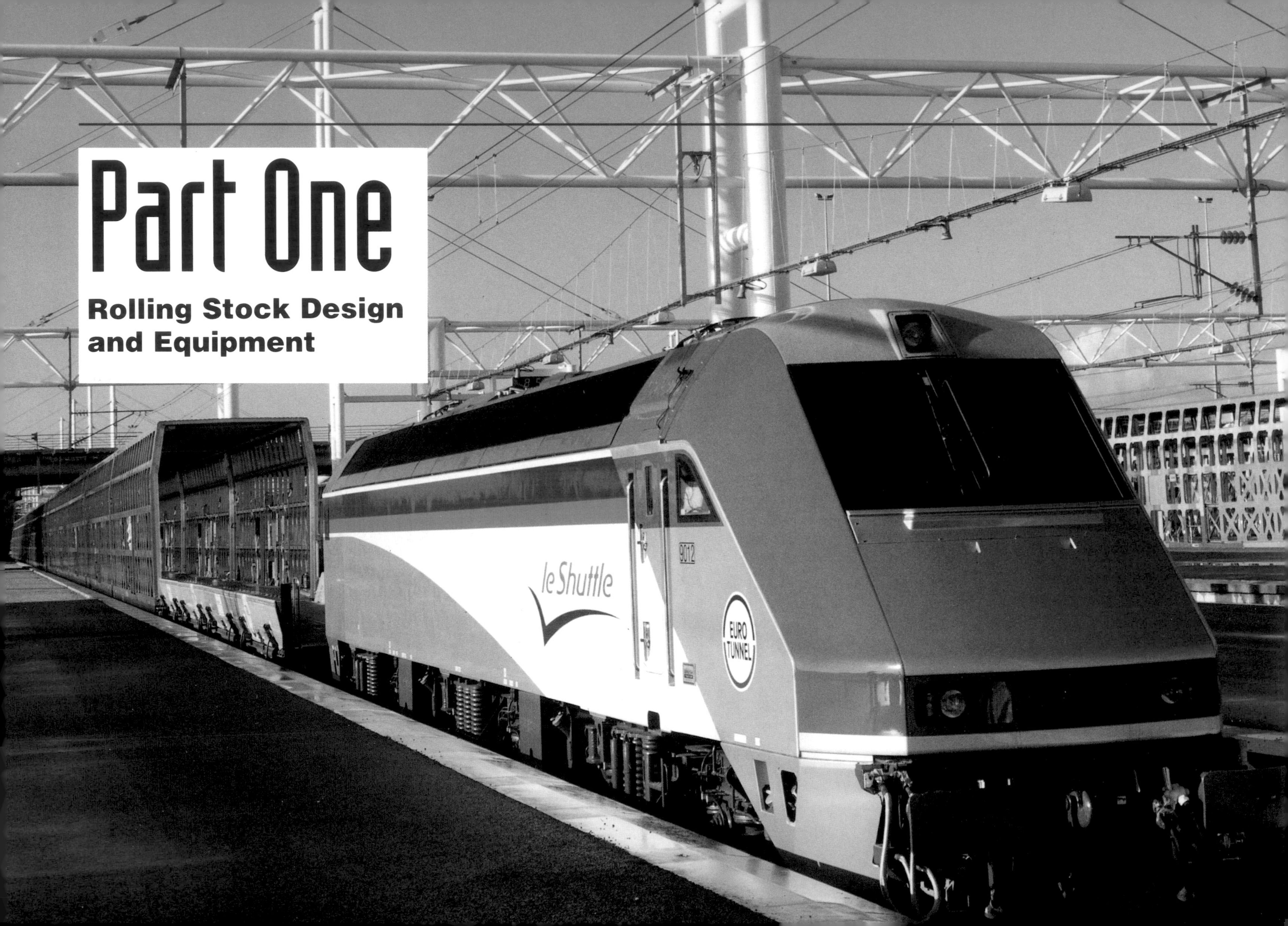

The Locomotive Fleet

There are two locomotives on each shuttle. The initial order was for 17 trains: nine passenger-vehicle shuttles and eight freight shuttles. These require 34 locomotives; four spares were added to make an initial order for 38 locomotives.

Design criteria

The shuttle locomotives have been designed to an extremely demanding performance specification. Each has to make some 20 single journeys a day, working trains of up to 2400 tonnes at speeds of up to 140km/h over gradients as steep as 1 in 90 in atmospheric conditions that can change rapidly from freezing outside the Tunnel to hot, with 100 per cent humidity, inside. The locomotives work in pairs, one at each end of the 750m-long train, controlled by the driver in the leading cab; in general, the locomotives share the traction effort equally.

Challenging though these requirements are, the design was conceived to cope with three critical emergency conditions. First, if a single bogie is isolated on one of the locomotives, they still have to be able to restart a train on the 1 in 90 gradient and accelerate it at 0.13m/sec². If one of the locomotives fails completely, the other must be able to restart the train on the maximum gradient and complete the journey at reduced speed. Finally, should an entire shuttle train fail completely, the next one must be able to push it out of the Tunnel. This requires each locomotive to have a power of at least 5MW (6700hp), with 132 tonnes of adhesion weight to ensure that the requisite high tractive effort can be maintained in the humid conditions of the tunnels. By using three-phase traction (see page 30), it proved possible to provide a continuous rating of 5.6MW (7500hp) within the maximum weight permitted.

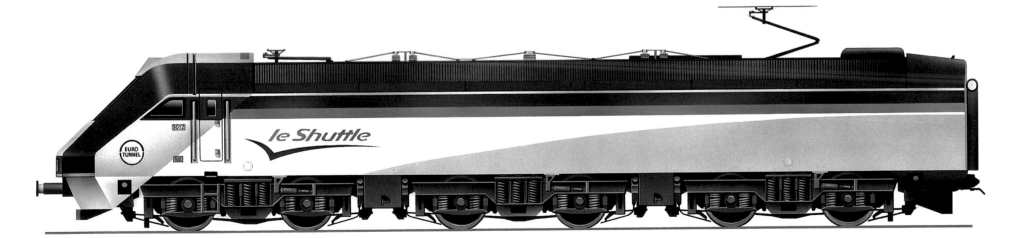

Locomotive in Le Shuttle livery

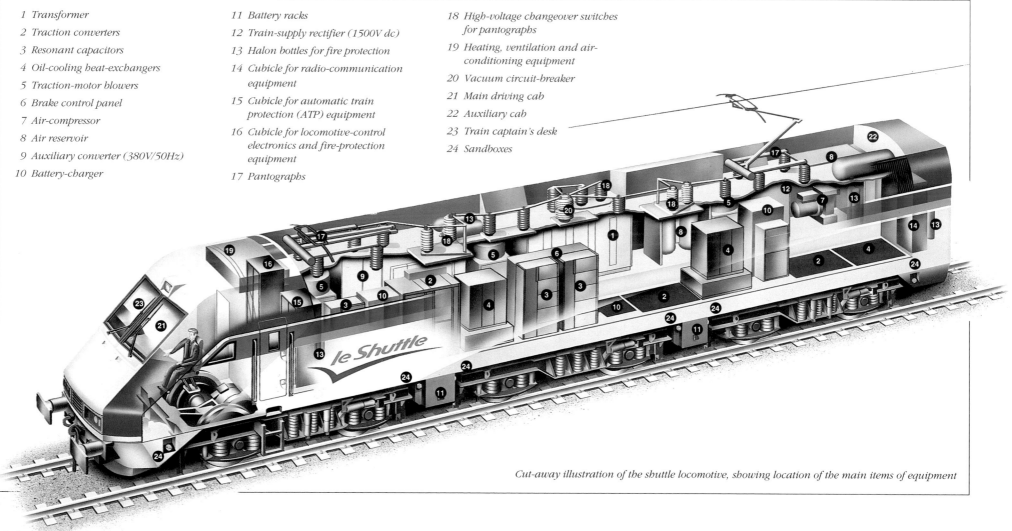

1 Transformer
2 Traction converters
3 Resonant capacitors
4 Oil-cooling heat-exchangers
5 Traction-motor blowers
6 Brake control panel
7 Air-compressor
8 Air reservoir
9 Auxiliary converter (380V/50Hz)
10 Battery-charger

11 Battery racks
12 Train-supply rectifier (1500V dc)
13 Halon bottles for fire protection
14 Cubicle for radio-communication equipment
15 Cubicle for automatic train protection (ATP) equipment
16 Cubicle for locomotive-control electronics and fire-protection equipment
17 Pantographs

18 High-voltage changeover switches for pantographs
19 Heating, ventilation and air-conditioning equipment
20 Vacuum circuit-breaker
21 Main driving cab
22 Auxiliary cab
23 Train captain's desk
24 Sandboxes

Cut-away illustration of the shuttle locomotive, showing location of the main items of equipment

The arrangement of the powered axles was another important design consideration. With a maximum permitted axle-load of 22.5 tonnes, the locomotive would require six axles. Using a pair of three-axle bogies would have produced the Co-Co wheel arrangement, a configuration already widely used, particularly for diesel-electric designs. However, the Co-Co configuration does not operate effectively on sharp curves and the loops in the two terminals have radii of only 280 to 500m. In such conditions, the angle taken up by the outer wheels on a long wheelbase bogie relative to the rails causes the flanges and the rails to wear, and reduces adhesion between wheel and rail. It was accordingly decided to adopt a three-bogie design, each with two axles, giving a Bo-Bo-Bo configuration. This provided a rigid wheelbase of only 2.8m, a reduction of about half, although the central bogie required a more complicated suspension system to provide lateral movement on curves.

There were other advantages. In modern locomotive designs all the motors on each bogie are normally fed by one supply system. With the Bo-Bo-Bo arrangement, if one set fails the locomotive loses only one third of its power, rather than half. The Bo-Bo-Bo configuration also reduces weight transfer between wheelsets, so enabling higher tractive efforts to be maintained under difficult conditions.

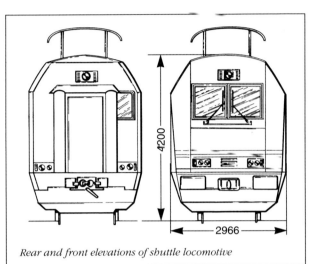

Rear and front elevations of shuttle locomotive

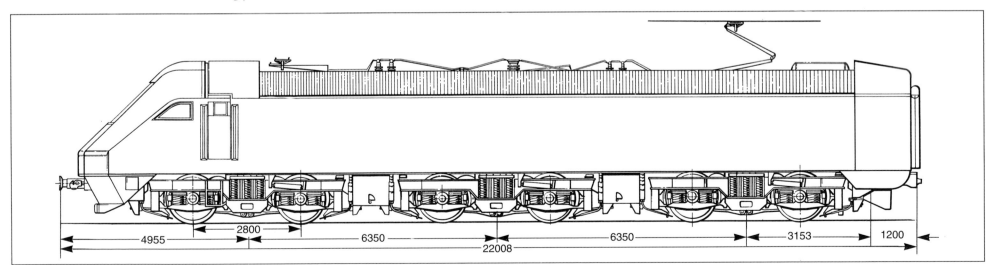

Side elevation of shuttle locomotive

When the shuttle locomotives were being designed in the late 1980s, the Bo-Bo-Bo axle arrangement was not used on main-line locomotives in either France or the UK. However, the Paris-Lyon *trains à grande vitesse* (TGVs) did effectively have this configuration, with three power bogies at each end of the set, two on each power-car and one under the outer end of the adjacent coach. A similar arrangement has been adopted for the Eurostar trains that will operate the passenger services through the Tunnel (see chapter 7). However, large numbers of three-bogie electric locomotives have been in use for many decades elsewhere, notably in Japan, Australia, Switzerland, Spain and Italy. In Italy, over 1700 were in service, many capable of 160km/h, but none of the designs was suitable for use on the shuttles.

Thus, since no existing locomotive fulfilled the Tunnel's requirements, it was decided to build new ones, using as far as possible equipment that had already been proven in operation. For example, ASEA Brown Boveri (ABB) could demonstrate 6MW Bo-Bo-Bo locomotives that had been operating through the Simplon and Gotthard Tunnels since 1972. In 1986 Brush Traction had begun delivery of 30 Bo-Bo-Bo locomotives for the New Zealand Railways; these had a rated output

Lowering the transformer into the first shuttle locomotive under construction in the Brush works in Loughborough. In the far right background is the mock-up of the shuttle locomotive, and two diesel-electric locomotives for Morocco are under construction on the left

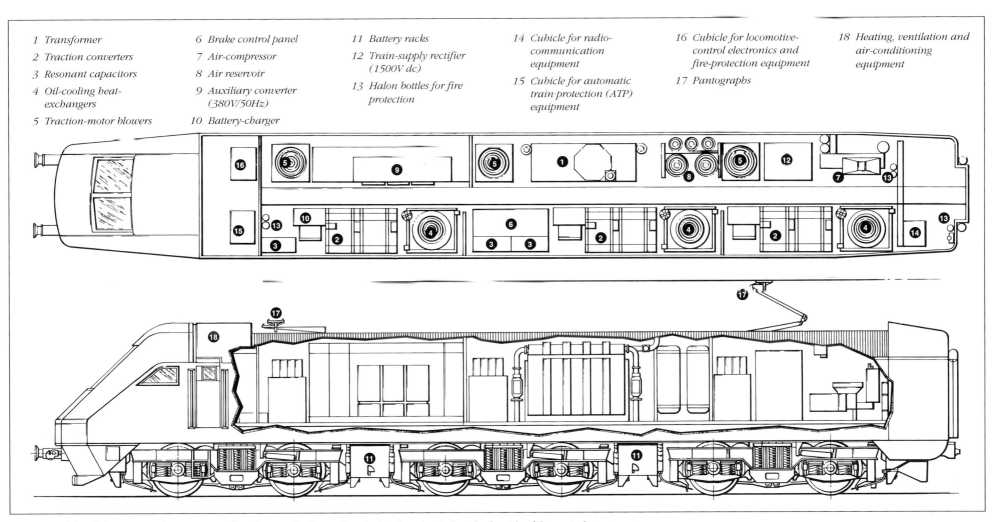

1 Transformer

2 Traction converters

3 Resonant capacitors

4 Oil-cooling heat-exchangers

5 Traction-motor blowers

6 Brake control panel

7 Air-compressor

8 Air reservoir

9 Auxiliary converter (380V/50Hz)

10 Battery-charger

11 Battery racks

12 Train-supply rectifier (1500V dc)

13 Halon bottles for fire protection

14 Cubicle for radio-communication equipment

15 Cubicle for automatic train-protection (ATP) equipment

16 Cubicle for locomotive-control electronics and fire-protection equipment

17 Pantographs

18 Heating, ventilation and air-conditioning equipment

Diagrams of shuttle locomotive showing items of equipment. The lower view depicts those located on the far side of the central passageway

of 3000kW (4020hp) in spite of operating on a gauge of only 1067mm (3ft 6in). Thus the mechanical parts of the Eurotunnel locomotives were built by Brush at their works at Loughborough, Leicestershire, based on the New Zealand locomotives, but suitably enlarged to take advantage of standard-gauge track and the UIC 505B loading gauge. Any major mechanical innovations that required testing were dealt with by the BR Technical Centre at Derby or the SNCF Technical Centre at Vitry. Despite their length (22m), The shuttle locomotives are considerably smaller than the shuttle wagons (4.2m maximum height above rail and 2.97m wide respectively compared with 5.6m and 4.1m). This permits the locomotives themselves to travel over main-line railways in continental Europe, so that future major overhauls can be carried out at any suitable locomotive works.

Like some other designs which operate in fixed formations, the shuttle locomotives are not symmetrical, having a sloping cab at one end and a blunt shape at the other, with a gangway connection to the train. The main driving cab is at the streamlined 'front' end. This cab also contains a train captain's position, although normally the train captain is based in the cab of the 'backwards'-facing rear locomotive, so permitting the train to be driven out of the Tunnel in that direction if necessary. A small cab at the train end of each locomotive can be used, at speeds limited to 80km/h.

Three-phase variable frequency drives

The development of the Gate Turn-Off (GTO) thyristor in the mid-1980s opened a completely new field of railway traction equipment, which has been exploited with great success. These devices are used in solid-state inverters, which, by varying the impulse time, turn a direct-current supply into a three-phase alternating-current supply on the locomotive. These permit three-phase traction motors to be used with simpler electrical controls and a reduced number of components.

The type of variable-frequency motor employed on the railways has several additional advantages over those used for constant-speed drives in industry. The output from the inverter is driven by a microprocessor and is in the form of variable-frequency ac, which is matched to the speed of the motors and hence that of the train, enabling the power output to be controlled very precisely. Although the TGV-Atlantique sets and the SNCF Class 26000 'Sybics' have synchronous motors, the majority of railway applications use the asynchronous, induction design, often called the 'squirrel cage' type. No power supply is needed for their rotors, which dispenses

with the need for a commutator or slip-rings, as well as brush-gear. This enables a longer rotor to be installed between the frames of a bogie, so increasing tractive effort.

The absence of any electro-mechanical commutation equipment reduces the possibilities of failure as well as decreasing routine maintenance. This is especially difficult to carry out when the motor is mounted in a bogie underneath a locomotive. Not only is an induction motor smaller, lighter and much more robust; it can even run at full voltage totally immersed in a bath of water!

Inverters can operate directly from the power collected from a dc third-rail electrification system such

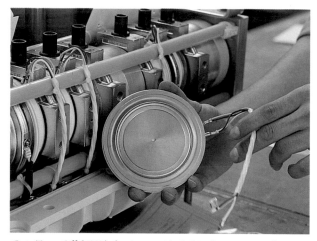

Gate Turn-Off (GTO) thyristor, with, behind, a semi-conductor assembly

as that used on many urban rail systems and on the tracks of Network SouthEast, whose new generation of 'Networkers' is equipped with this type of drive. However, trains working off a high-voltage ac system, such as the Channel Tunnel's 25kV, must first convert the power to a lower-voltage dc supply, using a transformer and thyristor bridges. This may seem a roundabout way of driving the motors, but in modern power electronics the only moving parts in the intermediate equipment are the cooling fans or pumps. These are required because thyristors belong to the family of devices known as 'semi-conductors', and thus have a higher electrical resistance than metals, this causes more heat to be generated when current is passing through them than through a metallic conductor. Every time the microprocessor turns the thyristor off, by affecting the polarity of its gate, the collapse of the field also produces heat; however, it is fairly easy to remove

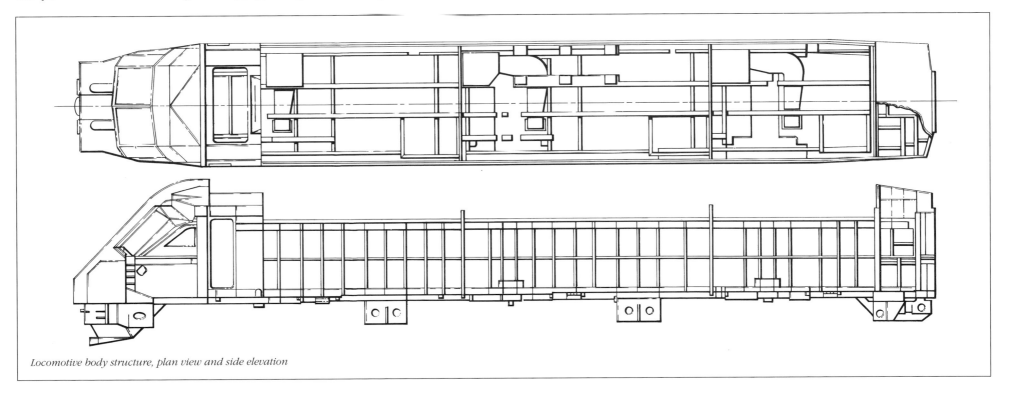

Locomotive body structure, plan view and side elevation

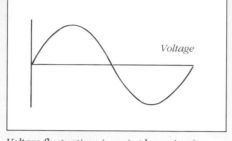

Voltage fluctuations in a simple ac circuit

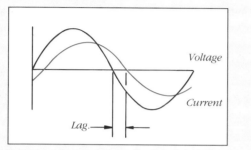

Voltage and current fluctuations in an ac circuit with inductance

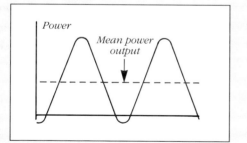

Fluctuation of power output in an ac circuit with voltage and power variations

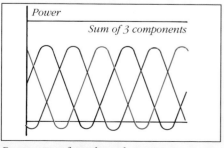

Power output for a three-phase motor

this using a suitable cooling system, because the actual losses are very low.

Using GTO thyristors for rail traction provides another important advantage for the Channel Tunnel. The electrical system can be reversed instantly, so that the motors generate electricity while 'braking'. The inverter then feeds the electricity back through the transformer into the overhead wires. This system, known as regenerative braking, enables the train to be slowed without causing wear and tear on the mechanical braking system. The power so produced can be used by other trains taking current from the same section of the overhead line, or is fed back into the national grid. While appreciable in itself, the energy saving also gives an indirect benefit. While heat and dust produced by brake blocks or disc pads will dissipate itself in the open air, in the depths of the tunnels it has to be removed by the cooling and ventilation systems, requiring a further expenditure of energy.

In a three-phase motor, the three individual power supplies combine to rotate their field at a speed related to the frequency, which is determined by the pulse of the GTO. The sum of the three separate phases from the inverters has a constant value. This is particularly important on railway locomotives, where the maximum amount of power has to be applied without causing the driving wheels to slip. The more even the torque, the higher the average power that can be applied.

This efficiency is achieved by the total symmetry of the power circuits between the transformers and motors. The input rectifier, which is also an inverter, feeds a constant-voltage direct-current circuit and, in turn, other inverters convert this direct current into alternating current for the three-phase traction motors. Capacitors in the intermediate dc circuit store energy and permit a constant inverter power-input to the traction motors, despite receiving pulsating primary power from the single-phase ac catenary supply. A power factor close to unity is thus achieved for both the traction and regenerative braking, and the very low 'interference currents' also prevent low-frequency harmonics affecting track signal circuits.

The locomotive body

The body shells for the shuttle locomotives were manufactured by Qualter Hall Engineering in Barnsley, South Yorkshire, and were fitted out in the Brush works at Loughborough. They consist of an all-welded monocoque structure, with fixed structural bulkheads. The body-sides are designed as complex deep beams whose high strength carries the vertical loads in addition to the longitudinal buffing ones, as shown in the illustration on page 19. The second body shell – without its roof in place – successfully underwent stress tests at BR's Technical Centre. These tests included simulating what would happen if a locomotive had to be jacked up on its diagonal corners; this action might be necessary to get it back on the track after a derailment in the Tunnel.

The roof structure, which contributes to the overall stiffness of the body, is constructed in three sections. These can be removed to permit easy access to the major internal items that have to be lifted out for attention. On the roof are mounted two pantographs and other electrical equipment, an air reservoir and Halon fire-extinguisher containers.

As with many modern electric locomotives, there are no windows to break up the sides of the bodies. A special technique was used to make the sides smooth and flat. Each is constructed from a single sheet of steel, 16m long, laid on a jig and subjected to a lengthways tension of 40 tonnes, which stretched it by 6 to 8mm. The various other structural members were then welded on, so that, when the assembly was released, the side panels remained stressed.

The main longitudinal members are situated at the floor and roof levels. Because of the large diameter of the wheels, some of the secondary structural components are positioned above the floor. The main power cables are contained in double-level trunking below the floor; the special fire-resistant cables fitted are stiffer than those used in conventional locomotives, thus further complicating their design. Above them, on a third under-floor level, are the various pipe-runs for compressed-air and oil-cooling systems. There is also special trunking for the control systems between the three electronic cubicles; this runs along the interior of the 'B' body-side (the right-hand side looking backwards from the front cab and along the central corridor ceiling).

The streamlined 'nose' of the locomotive is a resin/fibreglass fire-resistant moulding, from Strachan & Fox Composites of Westbury, Wiltshire. Cellobond FRP resins manufactured by BP Chemicals were used, which meet the fire safety standards required in the Tunnel. Each moulding weighs approximately 240kg, making it one of the largest items manufactured from this material, and is constructed to a tolerance of +/-2mm. The space between the nose moulding and the front metal bulkhead is filled with energy-absorbing honeycomb material to protect the driver in the event of a collision.

Inside the body of the locomotive the main equipment is arranged in a series of cubicles on each side of the central corridor that connects the cabs at each end. The cab at the front (No. 1 end) is full-width, with a cross-passage behind, leading to an exterior door on each side. On a twin-bogied modern locomotive the heavy and bulky transformer is normally mounted between the bogies on the underside of the body, but the Bo-Bo-Bo layout makes this arrangement impossible. However, because it was possible to reduce the size and width of the transformer, it could be mounted vertically on the 'A' side of the body (the left-hand side looking backwards from the front cab). The other equipment was carefully positioned to optimise weight distribution in the bogies.

The locomotive electronic cubicles in the cross-passage behind the front cab on the right side control and monitor the operation of the semi-conductor devices throughout the locomotive and provide a diagnostic system for fault-finding if anything goes wrong. On the other side are the solid-state tachometer and the TVM 430 automatic signalling systems.

An air-conditioning unit for the main cab is mounted in the roof above the cross-passage. This has a positive-displacement blower, rather than a fan, to reduce any pressure changes in the Tunnel which could discomfort the driver. Inflatable air seals are provided for the side and rear doors for the same reason.

Three identical sets of traction converters (inverters), together with their associated oil cooler groups, occupy most of the right side of the corridor (the 'B' side). Each converter supplies power to the pair of motors on the bogie beneath it. Heat generated in the semi-conductors is removed by a circulating oil system. The oil then passes through coolers, where air drawn by fans through inlets in the roof removes the heat, which is discharged beneath the locomotive. Such an arrangement prevents dust coming into contact with solid-state electronic components.

Also on the 'B' side of the corridor are three resonant capacitor cubicles containing equipment designed to prevent unwanted harmonics developing in the dc electrical circuits, since these can cause power loss and wave distortion. There is also the brake frame, on which are mounted the valves, relays and other equipment required to operate the electro-pneumatic air-braking system for the locomotive and train.

The other side of the corridor contains a variety of equipment, including the three traction motor blowers. Each of these axial-type vertical fans takes air from the roof inlets and forces it through the interior of the motors on one bogie to remove the heat produced by the current flowing through their windings. Separators mounted on the roof prevent water entering the cooling circuits; these have 97 per cent efficiency, even if the

The body of the second shuttle locomotive at Dover in December 1992, waiting on a road-trailer to travel to France by rail ferry

locomotive is standing under a lineside washing plant. Forward of the transfomer a long cubicle contains the equipment required to work the auxiliary electrical equipment on the locomotive. Below the rear pantograph is the corresponding equipment to provide the considerable power demand of the supply line to the train auxiliaries, with single-phase rectified current at 1500V dc.

The capacity of the rotary air compressor, which is mounted just in front of the rear cab, is larger than on a conventional locomotive. As well as providing power for the train's brakes, air is used by the pneumatic suspension equipment on the passenger-vehicle shuttle wagons. Because the atmosphere in the tunnels is extremely humid, as soon as air is compressed it becomes super-saturated. Twin driers are used to

Shuttle locomotive undergoing trials in the Czech Republic

The second shuttle locomotive, in works grey, stands in the entrance of the Calais maintenance building

remove any water that separates out of the compressed air as the pressure rises. Without this drying process, water would start to condense out, which would be a problem in small pipes, especially when the shuttle emerges from the relatively constant temperatures of the tunnel into a frosty winter's night. The twin driers are positioned alongside the transformer; one of the main air reservoirs is mounted on the rear of the roof, with two others inside the body near the transformer.

Opposite the controls in the cab at the No. 2 (rear) end is the communications cubicle. This houses the equipment that enables the train captain to keep in touch with the Control Centre (by radio) and to give passengers routine information about their journey as well as any special announcements (by radio and cable).

The interior of the locomotive is divided into four zones, each fitted with its own heat- and fire-detection systems. One of these consists of pressurised plastic tubing threaded through the different equipment cases. If any item overheats, the tubing melts and releases the air pressure, setting off an alarm in the cab. As soon as the alarm is activated, the power is shut off. If necessary, a Halon 1301 discharge is triggered to snuff out any fire, after allowing time for the ventilation fans to stop. The fire-fighting control equipment and small Halon bottles are located in two areas adjacent to each of the two cabs, with two larger Halon bottles on the roof.

A string of shuttle locomotives awaiting tests on the Calais Terminal

Dedicated hard-wired links running the length of the train connect the fire-alarm system in the rear locomotive to the display in the driver's cab in the front locomotive. There are also external manual controls for the extinguishers located in lockable cupboards on the outside of the shuttles.

Shuttle locomotive inside the Tunnel

Applying Le Shuttle livery to a locomotive

The bogies

Each locomotive bogie has a box-section frame, fabricated from steel plate. In plan view it is rectangular in shape, with a deep cross-member in the centre. The top plate of the bogie is machined from a single sheet of steel to avoid welds in critical places. A casting is attached to the bottom of each roller-bearing axle box, and this supports the pairs of coil springs which form the primary suspension. Inside each spring is a guide-post arrangement, with an intermediate rolling rubber ring, maintaining the alignment of the wheel-set with some resilience. Vertical dampers are provided on the ends of the mounting brackets.

Sets of three Flexicoil springs between the bogie and the dumb-bell-shaped bolster form the secondary suspension on each side of the bogie. Three vibration- and noise-dampening rubber-and-metal 'sandwich' stacks connecting the bolster with the underside of the body supplement the springs. A centre-pin locates the bolster, but does not handle the traction and braking forces; these are transmitted between the bogie and the locomotive body by two pairs of inclined rods positioned only about 200mm above the rails. This minimises the tendency of the bogie to tilt longitudinally, which would alter the weight-distribution on the two axles and affect the adhesion characteristics.

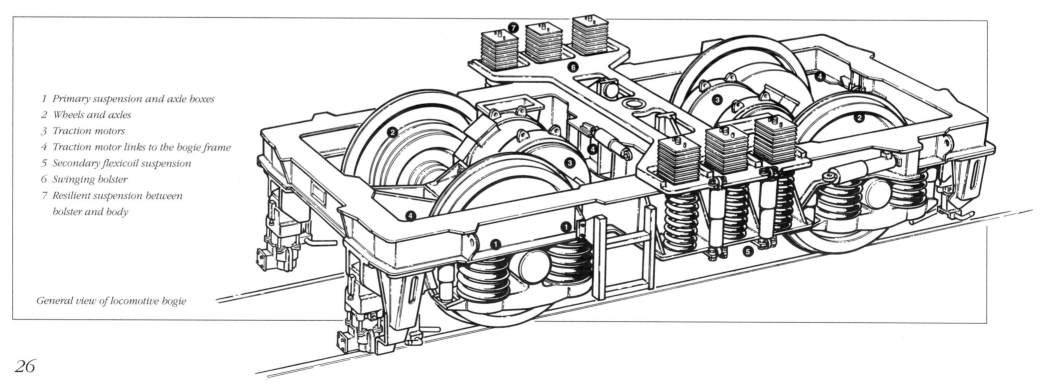

1 Primary suspension and axle boxes
2 Wheels and axles
3 Traction motors
4 Traction motor links to the bogie frame
5 Secondary flexicoil suspension
6 Swinging bolster
7 Resilient suspension between
  bolster and body

General view of locomotive bogie

Stops, operating in slots cut into the bolster, restrain the lateral movement of the bogies, although the central one is allowed a 200mm sideways movement in each direction to enable the locomotive to traverse sharp curves. In the depots, at slow speed, the locomotive can safely negotiate a curve with a radius as tight as 100m.

Each of the 960kW (1285hp) traction motors is bolted to the central cross-beam; this support is supplemented by a long bracket passing above the axles to the end of the bogie frame. In this way the motor is completely suspended and its weight is carried entirely by the primary springs. A drive system is required to enable the axle to move relative to the motor and gearbox This uses a hollow quill-shaft with cardan links surrounding

1 *Primary suspension and axle-box*
2 *Wheels and axle*
3 *Asynchronous traction motor*
4 *Links between motor and bogie frame*
5 *Cut-out of resilient mounting inside primary suspension*
6 *Motor pinion (V-shaped gear)*
7 *Main gear and drive links*
8 *Links to hollow shaft*
9 *Hollow shaft*
10 *Links from hollow shaft to wheel*

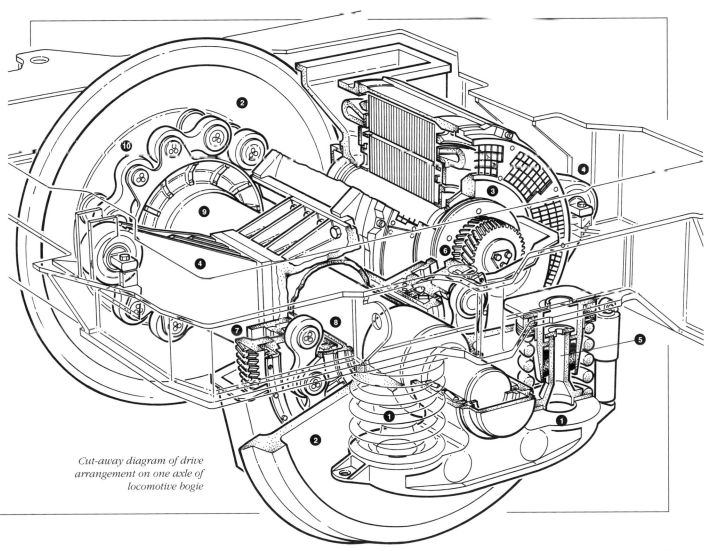

Cut-away diagram of drive arrangement on one axle of locomotive bogie

the axle. There are two cardan drives at each end of the shaft. Each consists of 3 + 3 flexible-link couplings which connect the shaft with the gearbox at one end and with the wheel web at the other. This enables the axle to move freely up and down relative to the power train over track irregularities. The gearbox and drive are derived from those provided by ABB for the 200km/h Class 120 electric locomotives for Deutsches Bundesbahn; the design originated from 4B (BB,BB) and 3B (BBB) diesel electric locomotives by R Mouneydière for CEM in France in association with the Swiss BBC Company (ABB). The teeth on the gear-wheels, made by Hurth, have a 'herring-bone' pattern to avoid any end thrusts on their shafts.

Pairs of conventional brake-blocks are applied to the tread of each wheel by individual air cylinders to provide mechanical braking; compensation is automatically made for wear. On each bogie two of the blocks also act as parking brakes, being applied by springs and released by air.

Power equipment

The locomotive collects power from the 25kV overhead contact wire by means of two Brecknell-Willis single-arm pantographs, each with metallised carbon strips on the upper surface of their heads. An air cylinder acting on the base of the lower arm keeps the pantograph in contact with the overhead wire, using small aerofoils to adjust it at speed to changes in the height of the wire. In the terminals the wires are particularly high above rail level to give maximum clearance, and the pantograph is designed to cope with this; conversely, when the locomotive enters the Tunnel, a beacon on the track activates a limit switch that stops the pantograph rising higher than 6.07m above rail level. (This applies to all locomotives and trains using the Tunnel.) This minimises damage to overhead equipment should the pantograph become 'dewired'.

Auto-Drop equipment is another in-built safety device. The channels supporting the carbon contact strips are pressurised with air from the cylinder that raises the pantograph. If one of the carbon strips breaks or wears through, the air is released and the pantograph lowers itself automatically.

Each locomotive normally uses one pantograph at a time. Aerodynamic tests showed that the best arrangement is for both shuttle locomotives to operate with their rear pantographs raised. Main-line locomotives with two pantographs generally do this as well, but for a different reason; if the leading pantograph hits an obstruction, debris could be carried back to damage the rear pantograph, so putting both out of action.

Primary suspension for locomotive wheel-set

Bogie secondary suspension

The high-voltage supply is carried from the pantograph along the roof in a standard roof line through the pantograph-isolating switches to the main circuit breaker (VCB). The circuit-breaker's contacts operate in a vacuum to prevent any arcing when it opens, either under the control of the driver or because of a short circuit. Under the latter conditions it could have to interrupt currents as large as 300 Megavolts-Amps (MVA). Situated before the circuit-breaker is the small auxiliary transformer; this operates the indicators in the cabs that tell the driver whether the overhead wire is energised, and at what voltage.

The high-voltage supply next enters the main transformer directly from the roof supply, passing through the primary winding to return to the feeder station via the wheels and rails. The transformer contains six traction secondary windings, two for each bogie; the electric supplies for each bogie are entirely separate from this point onwards, forming what is known as a 'traction bloc'. A switchable resonant

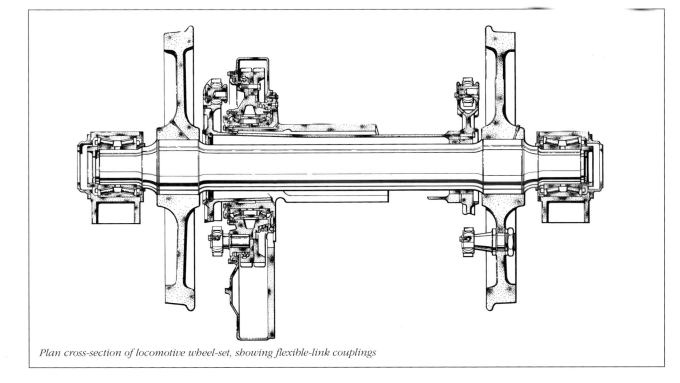

Plan cross-section of locomotive wheel-set, showing flexible-link couplings

Underside of locomotive bogie, showing rods that transmit the traction and braking forces to the body

Pantographs, lowered (above) and raised (above right)

capacitor is provided in each supply to avoid the production of unwanted interferences with other circuits in the Tunnel.

Each of the traction secondary windings feeds a pair of control or converter rectifiers, acting as four-quadrant converters to produce a reversible dc supply at the required voltage. Their operation thus determines the power output of the locomotive, and they are controlled by a microprocessor in response to the position of the driver's power lever. To ensure that the power

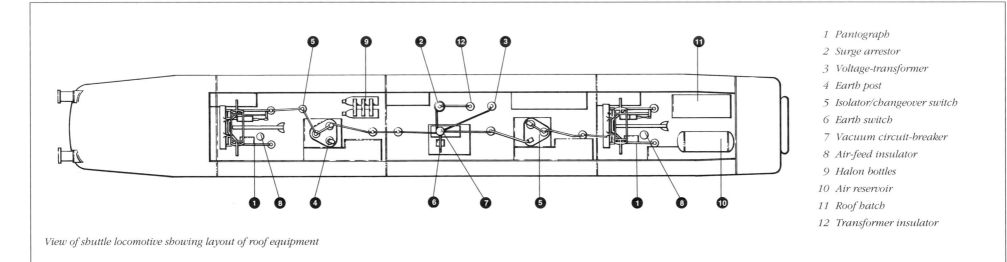

View of shuttle locomotive showing layout of roof equipment

1 *Pantograph*
2 *Surge arrestor*
3 *Voltage-transformer*
4 *Earth post*
5 *Isolator/changeover switch*
6 *Earth switch*
7 *Vacuum circuit-breaker*
8 *Air-feed insulator*
9 *Halon bottles*
10 *Air reservoir*
11 *Roof hatch*
12 *Transformer insulator*

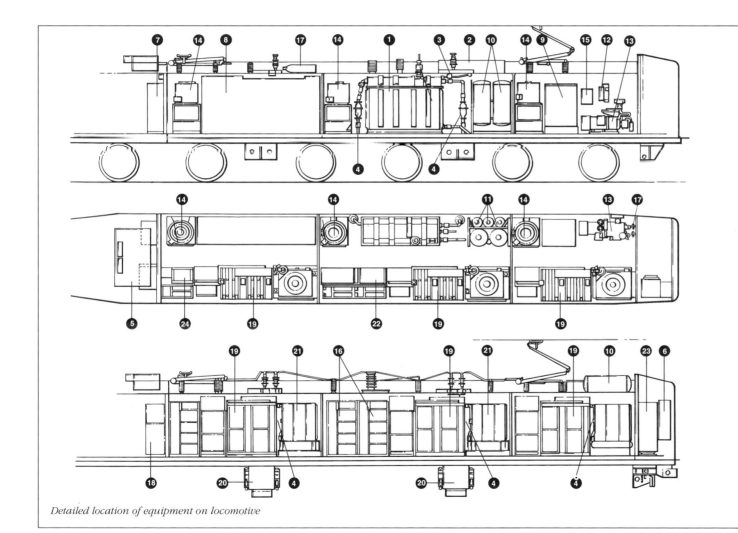

1 Transformer
2 Oil conservator tank
3 Buchholz relay
4 Coolant pump
5 Driving cab air-conditioning and equipment
6 Interface loco/train unit
7 Electronic power cubicle
8 Auxiliary converters cubicle
9 Train-supply rectifier cubicle
10 Main reservoirs
11 Auxiliary reservoirs
12 Air-drier
13 Air-motor compressor
14 Traction motor blower
15 No. 2 end pantograph panel
16 Resonant capacitor cubicle
   (dc intermediate circuit)
17 Fire-extinguishers
18 TVM 430 and speedometer control
19 Traction converters and coolers
20 Battery/sand boxes
21 Oil-cooler group
22 Brake equipment frame
23 Radio communications cubicle
24 Equipment cubicle

Detailed location of equipment on locomotive

One of the three main converter-units. The fibre-optic cables are in red

The central locomotive corridor with equipment panels closed

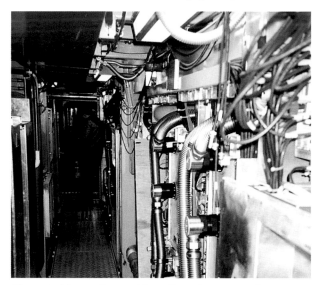

The central locomotive corridor with equipment panels open

equipment on each bogie is completely isolated if a fault develops, an earthing isolator is provided across the two dc power lines, before the smoothing and protection equipment.

The dc supply produced in this way is fed to the traction inverters, where the GTO thyristors produce a three-phase variable-frequency alternating supply to the field coils of the traction motors. These devices have no moving parts, no contacts and no fuses. The motors do not even need reversing contactors, reversing being achieved by instructing the GTOs to 'fire' in the reverse order, so that the electric field rotates in the opposite direction. To keep the various electrical circuits completely separate, and prevent unwanted induction effects, optical fibres carry the

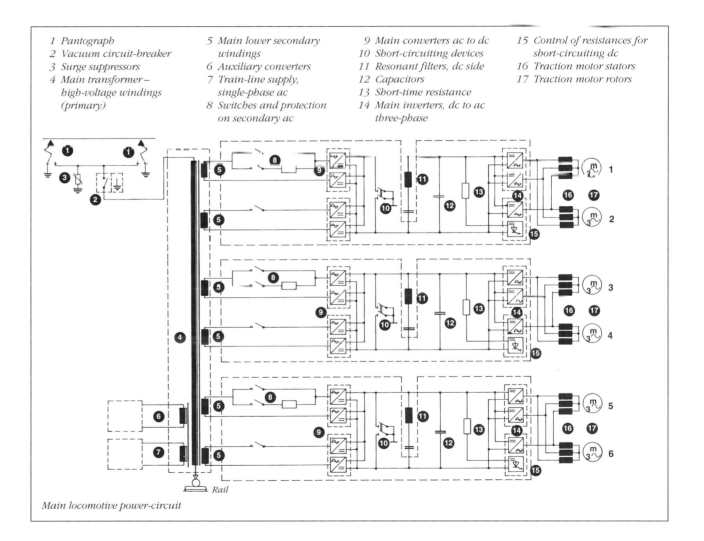

1	Pantograph	5	Main lower secondary windings	9	Main converters ac to dc	15	Control of resistances for short-circuiting dc
2	Vacuum circuit-breaker			10	Short-circuiting devices	16	Traction motor stators
3	Surge suppressors	6	Auxiliary converters	11	Resonant filters, dc side	17	Traction motor rotors
4	Main transformer – high-voltage windings (primary)	7	Train-line supply, single-phase ac	12	Capacitors		
		8	Switches and protection on secondary ac	13	Short-time resistance		
				14	Main inverters, dc to ac three-phase		

Main locomotive power-circuit

External view and cut-away (right) of vacuum high-speed circuit-breaker

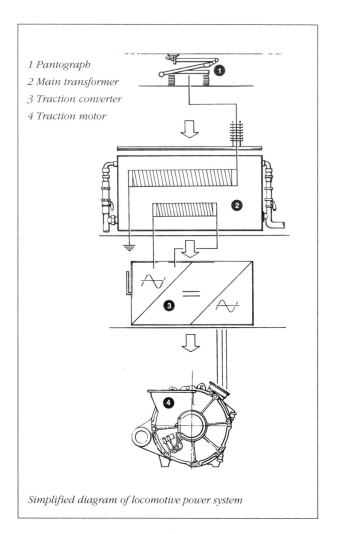

1 Pantograph
2 Main transformer
3 Traction converter
4 Traction motor

Simplified diagram of locomotive power system

microprocessor's control signals to the GTOs in analogue form.

As already mentioned, a three-phase induction motor of this sort is smaller and more than a third lighter than a corresponding dc traction motor (2.1 tonnes compared with 3.2 to 4.0 tonnes). It does not require a commutator or brush-gear, and all the interior parts can be fully insulated. There is the additional advantage that the whole system can be switched instantaneously to operate 'backwards' to regenerate power, thus braking the locomotive as well as supplying power for use by other trains.

Because the converters and inverters on the dc side include large capacitors that could still contain appreciable electrical energy even after the power has been turned off, interlocked switches are provided to ensure that they are earthed before the cabinet doors can be opened.

The results of this relatively complicated power electronic system are shown in the power diagram opposite, which also gives the tractive effort and braking curves for a locomotive as a function of its speed. From 0 to 20km/h, the maximum tractive effort per unit is limited to 400kN (90,000lbf) to avoid exceeding the adhesion limit between the wheels and the rails.

Between 20 and 65km/h another factor limits the maximum tractive effort; this is the maximum current that can be passed through the traction circuits. Above 65km/h the locomotive's rated output of 5.6MW can be sustained up to the maximum operating speed for which it is designed (176km/h). Although shuttle locomotives will not normally run at more than 140km/h at first, the specification calls for them to operate at 10 per cent above 160km/h, the highest they will work at in service.

Theoretically, if braking adhesion could be sustained at such levels, the maximum braking forces that can be produced by regeneration should be the same as those on the power side of the diagram. On the shuttle locomotives full advantage is not normally taken of this braking capability, the equipment being designed to provide a braking force of 190kN, which is maintained from 106km/h down almost to a stand still. When the driver uses the main brake lever, the application of the air-brakes on the locomotive is automatically 'blended' with the regenerative system to maintain a constant deceleration. Alternatively, moving the main power level backwards brings the regenerative brake alone into use; typically this is used to hold the speed constant on one of the long falling gradients under the Channel.

There are two other secondary windings on the

transformer, one to power the locomotive auxiliaries, and the other to provide the feed for the 1500V dc train supply. The total output of the latter, 750kW, has to be reduced as the locomotive passes through a neutral section, and this is controlled automatically from the wagons' converters, not from locomotive equipment.

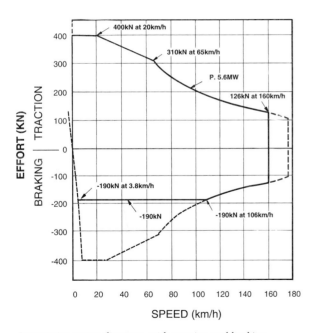

Locomotive power diagram, with tractive and braking efforts at different speeds

Lineside equipment causes the locomotive to 'notch back' its power output, at the same time reducing the output to the train line. As the neutral section is reached, the main circuit-breaker of the locomotive is automatically opened, and then closed again so that the power, fed by the other locomotive at a reduced level, can be ramped up. Even at full speed, the second locomotive at the rear of the train will not have to notch back until 20 seconds after the leading one, so that the reduction of power output to the train line will be smoothed out. The equipment on the passenger-vehicle shuttles is designed to cope with these virtually imperceptible power reductions. It is not necessary on freight shuttles because their power requirement is much less. The locomotive auxiliaries and the control circuits contain a number of new features not usual on BR and SNCF.

Braking systems

It is a vital part of the design of any train that the driver should be able to stop it in a given distance from its maximum design speed. For trains the size and weight of the shuttles, and carrying such a wide variation of loads, it is necessary to provide a combined electrical regeneration and mechanical system. The mechanical system involves normal brake shoes on wheels, operated using an electrically controlled servo-actuated pneumatic system. Priority is given to regenerative braking, in order to save energy and reduce the amount of heat generation, subject to the ability of the electrical system to receive the power.

The blending of regeneration and mechanical braking is achieved using a UIC approved brake control system that provides a continuously variable split between the two. A single lever controls the two systems on the locomotives and the air brakes on the shuttle wagons.

Both the passenger and the freight shuttle wagons rely on compressed air for the braking operation, and this provides the basic fail-safe system. Two air pipes run the length of the train. One, the air reservoir pipe, is used to charge the reservoirs on the underframe of each wagon with compressed air from the locomotives. Normally the pressure in the other air pipe, the air brake pipe, is controlled by the driver's brake valve; this is reduced to apply the brakes throughout the train, and restored to normal pressure to release them.

On each vehicle, the brake operation is controlled by a complicated valve called a distributor, which uses the changes in pressure in the brake pipe to regulate the flow of air from the reservoirs into the brake cylinders. This arrangement provides the 'automatic' safety system required by law to be fitted to every passenger train. Should the pipes between adjacent wagons be severed, the release of air pressure would immediately cause the brakes to be applied on both sections of the train. Non-return valves between the air reservoir pipe and the reservoirs ensure that the pressure in the reservoirs remains available to actuate the brake cylinders. As described on page 28, the cylinders force the pads on to the brake-discs mounted on the shuttle wagon axles.

There are also air-actuated brakes on the locomotives. However, the drives from the traction motor occupy the full length of the axles between the wheels, so there is no space for any discs and it was not desirable to fit them inside the wheel flanges. The air-brakes thus use traditional blocks applied to the wheel-treads. There are two per wheel, each being a totally enclosed unit consisting of an air cylinder and a slack-adjusting mechanism; this ensures that the brake does not lose its effectiveness as the blocks wear down.

If the wheel-set becomes locked while being mechanically braked, not only is braking efficiency reduced, but a 'flat' is also formed on the wheel-tread where the non-rotating wheel is dragged along the rail.

This subsequently causes a 'thump' each time the wheel rotates, making the journey noisier and less smooth as well as reducing wheel life. Most modern trains are fitted with elaborate wheel-slide devices; these quickly detect a wheel-set which is starting to slide and release the braking force progressively until the wheel starts to rotate normally again. On the shuttles these devices can detect an incipient wheel-slide and take action immediately, subsequently adjusting the brake pressure to the maximum sustainable under the prevailing adhesion conditions.

If a driver instigates a brake application by reducing the air pressure in the brake pipe, its propagation along the length of an 775m train would take a finite time, during which only the front portion of the train would have its brakes applied. To speed up the process and ensure that braking is applied evenly throughout the whole length of the train, the shuttles are provided with an electro-pneumatic (EP) system, brake applications and releases being made simultaneously throughout the train in response to electric signals sent along control wires. These are energised to keep the brakes released, so again the brakes are applied automatically if a wire is severed.

As already described, traction motors on the shuttle

locomotives provide regenerative electric braking. Normally, this is preferred to the air brake, since there is no frictional wear, and power is fed back into the wires. However, it is vital for the driver to be able to control the overall deceleration by means of a single brake-controller, which 'blends' the EP and regenerative brakes automatically. If contact is lost with the catenary for any reason, the air-brake system will take over entirely to bring the train to a stand still. Moving the locomotive's power controller towards the driver applies the regenerative brake alone; however, this is normally only used to restrain the train's speed on a falling gradient, while the main brake-controller is employed to reduce speed deliberately.

Air-operated brake-blocks on locomotive bogie

Two of the locomotive's brake cylinders incorporate a parking brake, which is applied by springs and released by air pressure. When the train is running with the main brakes released, the spring is not long enough to come into operation if the air supply holding the parking brake 'off' is lost. Parking brakes on individual shuttle wagons are applied by hand; these are only used when a rake of wagons is standing out of use in a siding.

Each shuttle locomotive is provided with an electrically-driven air-compressor. Unusually for British and French practice, it is of the single-stage rotary-screw type, capable of producing 3450 litres/minute. The drive is by a 50Hz three-phase 400V electric motor, so the machine runs at a virtually constant speed; this design was chosen because of its greater reliability and lower maintenance requirements.

Locomotive control systems

The complete control, regulation and diagnostic of the locomotive power system are handled by ABB MICAS Class S2 microcomputers, similar to those supplied for Swiss Federal Railways Class 450/460 locomotives and for the BT SZU railway.

For each two-drive motor unit, the system provides a separation between the overall locomotive control and the drive control level through the rectifier-inverter control itself. This also corresponds to the different software used for each level. The different drive units are linked by a common 'bus line', between motor drives, auxiliaries, pneumatic relays etc, the driver's console, the 'train line' connecting to the locomotive at the other end of the shuttle.

Many of the system duties, such as traction or braking action levels, wheel slip control and protection, power and speed characteristics, can be programmed on a pc basis. Similarly, diagnostic information can either be displayed or printed out for maintenance purposes, in the light of operational experiences.

The main bus line interconnecting microprocessors works on the basis of light signals and fibre-optic connections, to avoid any electromagnetic interference.

Cab layouts

The shuttle locomotives are normally driven from the large cab which occupies the full width of the front (No. 1) end. It has two seats, but the right-hand one – for the train captain – is not normally occupied during a journey; his or her position is in the locomotive at the rear of the shuttle train. Therefore it is only necessary to provide a sufficient physical separation between the two consoles to avoid any interference.

The driver's position is on the left, and he is provided with four main controls. On the right-hand side of the desk is the power controller, which is pushed forward to make the train move and accelerate. The direction of movement is previously determined by rotating the selector controller to 'forward' or 'reverse' Pulling the power controller back beyond the central or neutral position applies the regenerative brake only, which is also used to hold the speed constant on descending gradients. To reduce speed, the driver uses the main brake controller on the left-hand side of the desk. This applies the air brakes along the train as well as the locomotive's regeneration equipment; the control system automatically blends the two systems to optimise retardation, using the regeneration facility to regain as much energy as possible. Further to the left is the lever that applies the direct air-brake on the locomotive when it is running by itself.

These four are the basic controls needed to operate a train. Other controls include the signalling system which gives the driver authority to move and indicates the authorised speed levels (see chapter 11). Much other detail is presented on a visual display unit, its various

1 Main traction and braking control lever

2 Double-tone horn

3 Electro-pneumatic and direct braking

4 Reverser and locking key

5 Automatic speed control on/off switch

6 Information and diagnostics screen

7 TVM 430 – speed control

8 Radio coding keyboard

9 Speed selection knob

10 Button to initiate automatic starting sequence

11 Radio (combined console also used by train captain)

12 Handle for sun-screen curtain

13 Emergency pantograph lowering

14 Stand-by push button

15 Information and diagnostic keyboard

16 Miscellaneous control switches

17 Parking brake push-button

18 Brake pressure-gauges

19 Lighting and air-pressure gauge conditioning switches

20 Driver's safety device pedals

21 Locomotive brake isolator

22 Brake test and release button

23 Train captain's touch-screen keyboard

24 Video screens for shuttle wagon supervision

25 Train captain's console and door controls

26 Fire-detection and -activation systems

27 Sanding push-button

28 Pantograph manual pre-selection

29 Screen-wiper switch

30 Tractive and braking effort ratio indicator

31 Speedometer

32 Pneumatic manual switches

33 Cab temperature control

Diagram of main driving cab showing controls and instruments

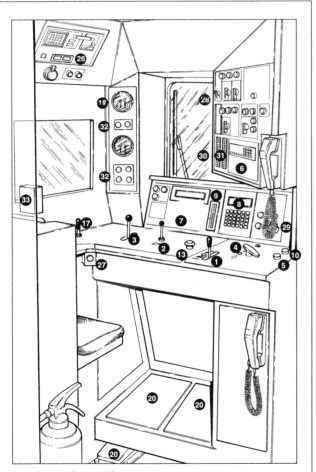

Auxiliary cab controls

buttons on a keyboard enabling a particular set of information to be selected. This replaces many other instruments. Diagnostic fault-finding is included, although some failures trigger their own warning lights on the panel. To minimise any language problems, pictograms are used to identify most of the switches. Other important sets of equipment are the fire panel on the upper side on the left of the driver, with detection lights and fire-fighting switch on its own keyboard.

The lay-out of the cab has been optimised to make the task of driving the trains as stress-free as possible. The controls can be used by a wide range of differently sized drivers; in addition, to cater for both British and continental practices, the driver can operate either sitting or standing. Another important design feature is the restriction of the driver's lateral view, to stop 'segment

flicker'. Since the early days of fast electric and diesel trains, care has had to be taken to ensure that the rapid passage of sleepers does not mesmerise a seated driver. In the tunnel, passing the all-embracing 1.5m-long tunnel segments at speed could create the same effect, and so a similar all-round restriction has been imposed on the driver's field of vision.

Normally the small cab at the No. 2 end is only used for slow-speed shunting operations, although occasionally it may be needed if a locomotive has to be driven 'backwards' through the Tunnel by itself; under such conditions special speed restrictions apply. The locomotive can also be controlled from one of the small cabs on the outer ends of the shuttle loading wagons, as well as by radio control from the ground alongside in the terminals; this facility is used at very low pre-selected

Horn controls	*Raise pantograph on locomotive No. 2*	*Parking brake control*	*Cab light control*	*Socket for hand-lamp*

Examples of pictograms from the locomotive cab

speeds when a group of wagons is being positioned inside the maintenance facility with the locomotive attached.

The train captain, who normally travels in the right-hand seat of the main cab of the rear locomotive, is responsible for supervising the shuttle wagons and their passengers, as well as for passing messages to them and crew members, and for dealing with emergencies. A range of monitors and controls is provided. In the centre of the captain's desk are two main screens which can be switched to any of the closed circuit-cameras in the shuttle wagons. Touch screens on each side of the

screens enable the train captain to select whatever set of information is currently required, in an emergency as well as under ordinary conditions. Pre-recorded and one-off announcements can be made to any part of the train via the visual and audio equipment in the shuttle wagons. Should a train, or half-train, have to be reversed out of the tunnel, the train captain, who is also trained as a driver, changes seats and operates the train.

A static mock-up of the cab is displayed in the Eurotunnel Exhibition Centre at Folkestone. For training purposes Eurotunnel possesses two fully operational driving simulators. Their controls are linked to a

computer that produces the correct responses to the actions of the driver. The responses are fed back to the appropriate instruments in the cab, and also control the visual display of the track ahead, which consists of computer-generated images seen through the 'windscreen'. The instructor's monitoring system can also be used to introduce abnormal occurrences, so that drivers and train captains can practice their responses to such situations. These simulators are similar to those used by drivers of the Eurostar trains.

Driver's view in the cut-and-cover section of the Tunnel (see chapter 8) near the UK portal

Driver's and train captain's (right) views from the cab in the Calais terminal maintenance area

Couplings

The front end of each shuttle locomotive is fitted with a standard UIC screw coupling and heavy-duty buffers. These enable any locomotive with a UIC coupler, such as Eurotunnel's diesel-electrics (see chapter 7), to tow a stranded train to the end of its journey. A shuttle train can also couple on to a stranded international night

Fish-eye interior view of the auxiliary cab at the train end of the locomotive

1 Rotating coupling nose
2 Casing
3 Uncoupling cylinder
4 Latch
5 Latch release
6 Rotor lug
7 Coupling indent
8 Rotating coupling
9 Stop
10 External positioning nose

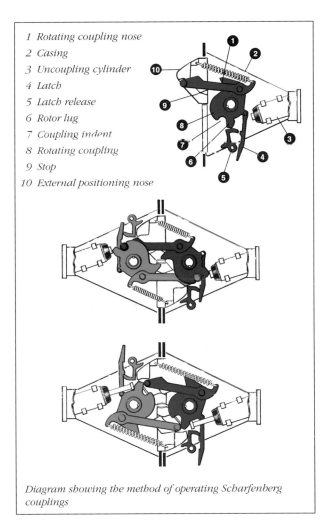

Diagram showing the method of operating Scharfenberg couplings

passenger or freight through-train. (These freight trains may be powered by a single class 92 locomotive, giving less overall 'redundancy' in their power supply equipment than other types of train using the Tunnel; statistically, therefore, they are more likely to require assistance from time to time.) The UIC front coupling on the shuttle locomotives was adopted for this reason.

At its other end, the shuttle locomotive is equipped with a very specialised Scharfenberg coupler that allows it to couple and uncouple from a train automatically. As well enabling the locomotive to haul the train, this coupler also connects the air-brake pipes and the main electrical power line to the wagons, together with some 200 separate control circuits. Similar couplers are used at the ends of each group of three passenger-vehicle shuttle wagons (triplets, see chapter 2), and of the loading wagons.

The firm of Scharfenberg has been making automatic couplers for nearly 100 years. This shuttle version is particularly complicated, as all the information and control circuits pass through it, as well as the 1500V train line providing power to the shuttle wagons. In addition, one of the circuits also enables the driver to control the operation of the locomotive at the rear of the train, using a Time-Division Multiplex (TDM) system.

In the absence of side buffers, the coupling on a railway vehicle has to transmit the traction, braking and buffing loads during the journey. An automatic coupling must engage securely as the two vehicles it links are moved slowly together. The crew must also be able to release the coupling in order to divide the train; if part of a train were immobilised in the Tunnel, the remainder would be uncoupled to continue on its journey. In the Tunnel, uncoupling must take place without any of the train crew getting out of the train – the entire Tunnel ventilation system has to be reconfigured before this is permitted.

The basic principle of the Scharfenberg coupler is shown in plan view on page 41, where it is in the 'open' position, ready to join up with another. The vital components are the conical nose, the coupling arm and the rotor. Each coupling arm consists of two specially shaped steel plates, mounted parallel with each other and joined by a roller working on a vertical axis at the end. As the two vehicles come together, the end of this arm engages the lug on the rotor of the opposite coupler, making both rotors turn anti-clockwise. After rotating through nearly 90 degrees, the rollers engage with the indents, providing a double mechanical connection between the two vehicles.

When the coupler is 'open', the rotor's position is held by the latch, one of whose indents engages on the outer casing. As the two vehicles come together, the couplers, which have a limited lateral movement to cope with curves on the track, are aligned by the angled 'horns' on their bottom faces. When the nose comes into contact with the latch release on the opposite coupler, it disengages the latch, enabling the rotor to turn anti-clockwise. The rotation is stopped when the rotor nose comes into contact with the stop. The profile of the coupling arms is designed to position the ends laterally as they move in and out through the slot in the casing. They are held wide apart as the couplers meet but, when engaged, the rollers are prevented from moving sideways out of the indents.

To uncouple two wagons, both rotors have to rotate clockwise to release the coupling arms from the indents. To do this the lugs on one or both of them are pushed round by the rams from the uncoupling cylinders. As the rotors turn, the latch is engaged by the latch release, which prevents the couplers re-engaging when the air is exhausted from the uncoupling cylinders. As the two vehicles separate, the withdrawal of the nose frees the latch release. This then moves anti-clockwise, letting the latch re-engage with the casing. The coupling is then back to its normal 'open' position, ready for the next marshalling operation.

Air to the uncoupling cylinders is supplied from the reservoir air pipe via special valves on both vehicles. The ends of the small connecting pipe between the two cylinders are mounted in the centre of the face of the coupling, right at the bottom, as shown in the photographs. In an emergency one of the rotors can be rotated mechanically from inside the vehicle, thus initiating the uncoupling operation even if an air supply is not available.

On the shuttles, connections between the main train air pipes are made automatically on the face of the coupler as a pair of vehicles is pushed together. As mentioned above, many other vital connections also have to be made. To do this, air cylinders gently force the side boxes of contacts together after the main coupling has engaged. The left and right halves are mirror images of each other, one side having 'male' contacts, the other the corresponding 'female' ones.

The majority of the 200 pairs of contacts have to handle quite small voltages and currents. The main exception is the pair in the outer top corners, which connect the 1500V dc supply from the locomotives to provide power for the equipment on the wagons.

Locomotive coupling in unlocked position

On the locomotives the Scharfenberg couplers are in the standard UIC position, with their centre-line at a height of 1025mm above the rails. In contrast, on the passenger-vehicle shuttle wagons, they are positioned only 680mm above rail level to provide maximum internal headroom for road vehicles. As a result, the two sets of couplers on the loading and unloading wagons at the end of each shuttle are at different heights, to engage with those on the locomotive and the adjacent shuttle wagon.

A semi-permanent type of coupler is used between the HGV shuttle wagons, as well as within the passenger-vehicle shuttle triplets. The club car used on the HGV shuttles, marshalled between the locomotive and the loading vehicle, also has UIC-height Scharfenberg couplers at both ends.

The Passenger-Vehicle Shuttle Fleet

Each passenger-vehicle shuttle consists of two separate halves, or rakes, single-deck and double-deck. The single-deck half contains two loading/unloading wagons and twelve carrier wagons. The double-deck half contains two loading/unloading wagons and twelve carrier wagons. All shuttles have a locomotive at each end.

Eurotunnel's initial order was for nine passenger vehicle shuttles. The total fleet is therefore:

18 single-deck loading/unloading wagons plus one spare

18 double-deck loading/unloading wagons plus one spare

108 single-deck wagons

108 double-deck wagons

Wagon design

The wagons that form the shuttle trains are the largest railway vehicles in the world. They occupy over half the cross-sectional area of the Tunnel, where they travel for 50km at speeds of up to 140km/h. Such speeds cause rapid changes in the external pressure, and so sophisticated systems and equipment have been provided to prevent these fluctuations making the journey uncomfortable for passengers and to ensure their safety in the world's longest undersea tunnel.

Each passenger-vehicle shuttle train is 776m long, and consists of 28 wagons and two locomotives.

The passenger-vehicle shuttle wagons were built by the Euroshuttle Wagons Consortium (ESCW). This was composed of GMT-Bombardier (Canada), La Brugeoise (BN) (Belgium) and ANF Industrie (France). These are all now subsidiaries of Bombardier Eurorail, which sub-contracted the construction of the 508 bogies required to GEC-Alsthom at its Le Creusot works. The two spare loading wagons were ordered directly by Eurotunnel in 1990.

Single-deck passenger-vehicle wagon

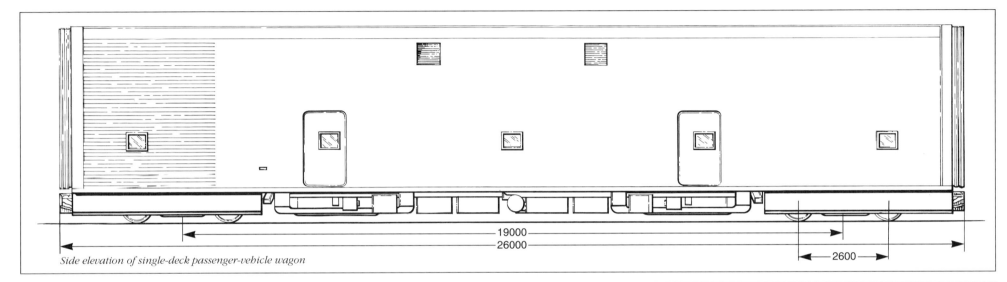

Side elevation of single-deck passenger-vehicle wagon

19000
26000
2600

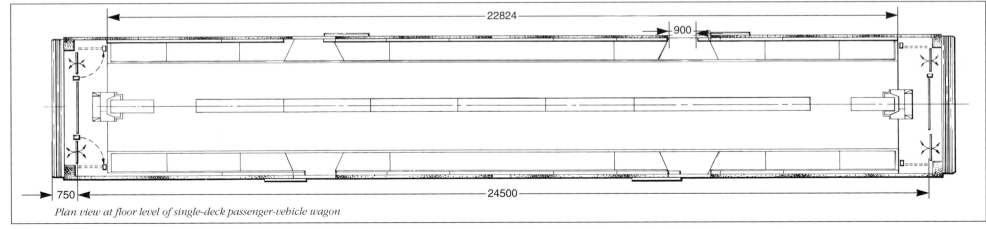

22824
900
750
24500

Plan view at floor level of single-deck passenger-vehicle wagon

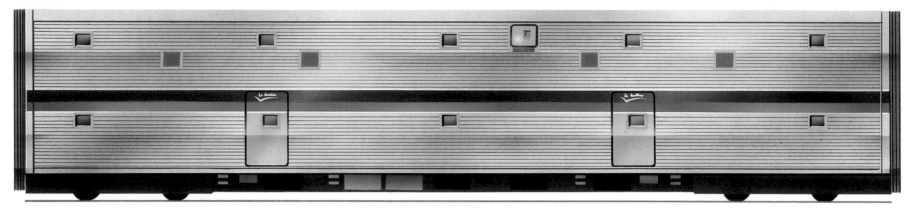

Double-deck passenger-vehicle wagon

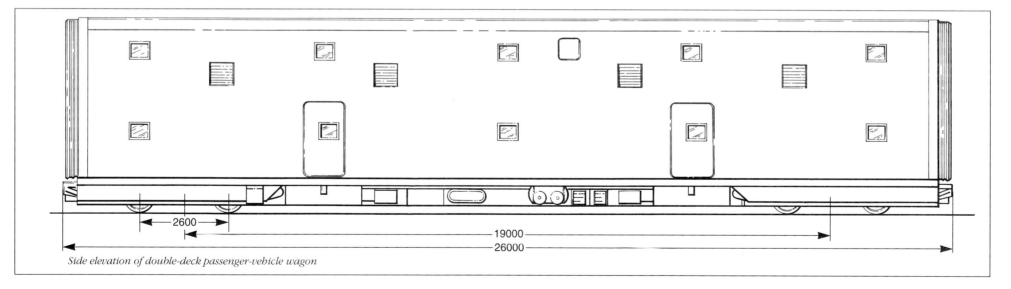

2600

19000

26000

Side elevation of double-deck passenger-vehicle wagon

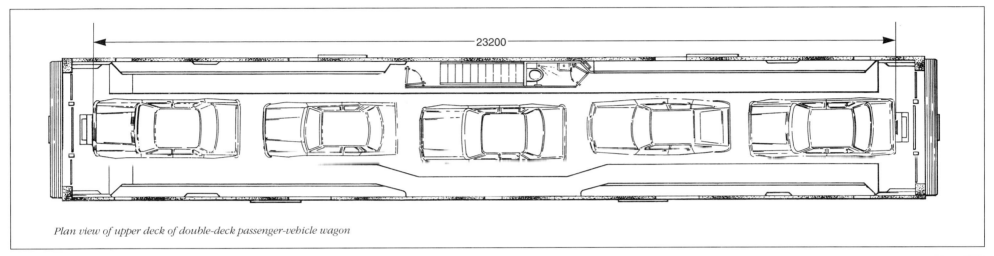

Plan view of upper deck of double-deck passenger-vehicle wagon

23200

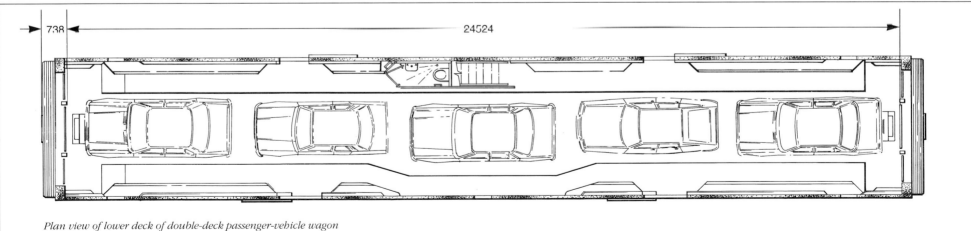

Plan view of lower deck of double-deck passenger-vehicle wagon

738   24524

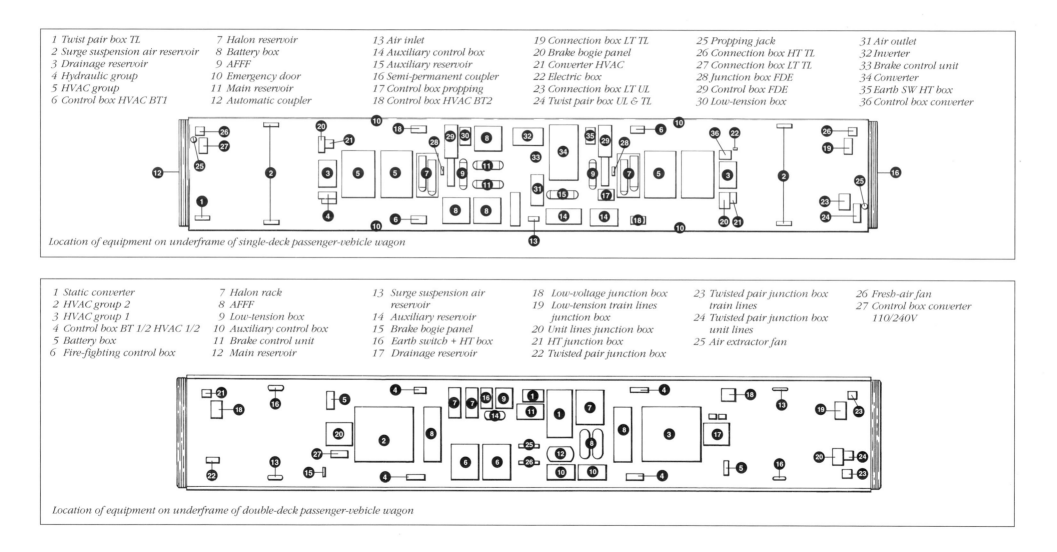

1 Twist pair box TL
2 Surge suspension air reservoir
3 Drainage reservoir
4 Hydraulic group
5 HVAC group
6 Control box HVAC BT1

7 Halon reservoir
8 Battery box
9 AFFF
10 Emergency door
11 Main reservoir
12 Automatic coupler

13 Air inlet
14 Auxiliary control box
15 Auxiliary reservoir
16 Semi-permanent coupler
17 Control box propping
18 Control box HVAC BT2

19 Connection box LT TL
20 Brake bogie panel
21 Converter HVAC
22 Electric box
23 Connection box LT UL
24 Twist pair box UL & TL

25 Propping jack
26 Connection box HT TL
27 Connection box LT TL
28 Junction box FDE
29 Control box FDE
30 Low-tension box

31 Air outlet
32 Inverter
33 Brake control unit
34 Converter
35 Earth SW HT box
36 Control box converter

Location of equipment on underframe of single-deck passenger-vehicle wagon

1 Static converter
2 HVAC group 2
3 HVAC group 1
4 Control box BT 1/2 HVAC 1/2
5 Battery box
6 Fire-fighting control box

7 Halon rack
8 AFFF
9 Low-tension box
10 Auxiliary control box
11 Brake control unit
12 Main reservoir

13 Surge suspension air
   reservoir
14 Auxiliary reservoir
15 Brake bogie panel
16 Earth switch + HT box
17 Drainage reservoir

18 Low-voltage junction box
19 Low-tension train lines
   junction box
20 Unit lines junction box
21 HT junction box
22 Twisted pair junction box

23 Twisted pair junction box
   train lines
24 Twisted pair junction box
   unit lines
25 Air extractor fan

26 Fresh-air fan
27 Control box converter
   110/240V

Location of equipment on underframe of double-deck passenger-vehicle wagon

The passenger-vehicle shuttles, which are sometimes also known as tourist shuttles, have two types of wagon. The double-deck (DD) wagon is designed for cars with a maximum height of 1.85m. The single-deck (SD) wagons are used by cars with high trailers or roof racks, coaches, minibuses, and other larger vehicles more than 1.85m high. Both types are 26m long, with a height of 5.6m above rail level. They are designed for a maximum speed of 160km/h, although initially they will operate at 140km/h. Each single-deck wagon weighs 63 tonnes

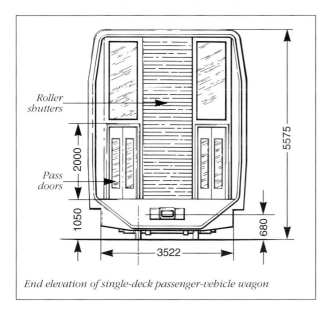

End elevation of single-deck passenger-vehicle wagon

Single-deck passenger-vehicle wagon under construction

empty; double-deck wagons are 2 to 4 tonnes heavier because of the extra floor.

The wagons are made of stainless steel. All their structures and fittings are built to provide the best insulation against noise and thermal variations during their operational life. Insulation, in particular with fire-resistant rock-wool materials, ensures a noise level of less than 80dB.

Both types of wagon are formed into half-trains, or rakes, as loading wagon – 12 carrier wagons – unloading wagon. A complete passenger-vehicle shuttle will normally operate as a single-deck and double-deck rake

End view of double-deck passenger-vehicle wagon. Note that the bellows enclose the couplings

Loading on to the lower deck of a double-deck shuttle

together, coupled to two locomotives, one at each end.

Carrier wagons

Each single-deck wagon can carry any combination of vehicles weighing up to a total of 24 tonnes. Each deck in a double-deck wagon is designed to support a total load of up to 12 tonnes; this is sufficient to take five conventional cars. For all carrier wagons, the maximum rail-axle load is under 22 tonnes.

Two slightly different designs of SD and DD wagons – 'A' and 'S' – have been built. These are coupled semi-permanently into 'triplets' in the formation 'A-S-A'. From the user's point of view, the only difference is that double-deck 'S' wagons have a passenger stairway in the middle and toilets on both decks. (There is no space for toilets in SD carrier wagons; they are located instead in the loading/unloading wagons.) The coupling arrangements of each design also differ (see chapter 1). When a train is being marshalled for service, triplets can be added or removed by ordinary shunting movements, normally using the automatic low-level couplers on their outer ends. However, because the individual wagons within a triplet are joined by a semi-permanent bar-coupling, they can only be separated and joined by maintenance staff. A half-shuttle consists of four triplets (and thus twelve wagons) together with a loading wagon at each end.

Shuttle locomotive with single-deck passenger-vehicle rake

View along the interior of a single-deck rake

Interior of a double-deck carrier wagon, with the fire door closed

When road vehicles enter the shuttle they drive along a continuous flat floor; side kerbs, 92mm high on DD and 150mm high on SD wagons, prevent them getting too near the walls. Floor plates bridge the gap between each carriage just above the couplers, enabling vehicles to drive along the half-shuttle from one end to the other during loading and unloading operations. There are separate routes through on both levels of the double-deck wagons. Air-tight 'bellows' enclose all the space between the wagons, including connecting bridges and couplers, and are designed to ensure that sudden changes of air pressure in the Tunnel do not affect passengers. Their size and fire-resistance capabilities makes them unique in the railway world.

The door systems that close off the wagon ends consist of two side-sections hinged from the wagon side with a descending roller shutter between them; they were made by De Dietrich in France. When these are in place and the seals between them have been inflated, the whole door assembly becomes a barrier capable of resisting a fire inside the wagon for up to 30 minutes, long enough for the shuttle to reach either end of the Tunnel. Passengers may use pass doors in each hinged section to reach the toilets in the central 'S' wagon of each double-deck triplet, or those at the ends of the SD loading wagons. The opening of these pass doors is hand-operated, using a push button with a two-second delay.

Air-operated steel protection arms, rising out of the floor near the ends of the wagons, prevent vehicles colliding with the fire doors, should the handbrake on the car nearest a door be insufficiently applied or accidentally released.

Le Shuttle staff guide each vehicle into position and ensure that the hand brake is on. When the wagon is full, they close the doors and shutters between wagons, and raise the steel protection arms.

Normally, passengers drive off the shuttles in their vehicles. Two emergency doors are provided on the walkways on each side of each wagon for use should it ever be necessary to evacuate a shuttle in the Tunnel. These doors are normally locked, but can be unlocked pneumatically by the train captain and also locally if the shuttle speed is below 5km/h. If the normal mechanism cannot be operated, manual opening is also possible in an emergency if the shuttle has stopped. Passengers would alight on to the continuous walkway on the side nearest the service tunnel.

Stabilisers

When heavy vehicles drive on to, along or off the shuttles, they could cause unacceptably large deflections in the wagons' suspension system as their centre of gravity moves. To prevent this happening, stabilising beams or jacks are provided under those wagons that have to handle heavy loads.

Stabilising beams are fitted to freight and to single-deck passenger-vehicle carrier wagons to resist the longitudinal forces caused by heavy vehicles driving along inside the shuttles. There are two beams per wagon, each operated by two hydraulic pistons. The beams hinge down across the two rails of track, and lift the wagon slightly off its suspension.

Floor joint between two carrier wagons with the fire doors open

Stabilising jacks are provided on freight and single-deck passenger loading/unloading wagons to resist the transverse forces caused by heavy vehicles loading. The possible forces are too great for the track to resist, so concrete beams have bean cast alongside the track. There are six jacks, of two different types, which locate on these beams and lift the wagon slightly off its suspension.

There are no beams or jacks on the double-deck shuttles, since the loads created by cars are much less.

Loading/unloading wagons

A loading/unloading wagon is positioned at both ends of each half-shuttle. Vehicles drive in through the rear loading wagon and drive out through the front unloading wagon. The two types of loading wagon differ considerably in design.

Double-deck loading wagons

Externally, DD loading wagons closely resemble carrier wagons, although the window arrangements differ. Two large sliding doors, 6m long, on each side let vehicles drive in and out. Cars entering and leaving the lower deck use the doors nearer the carrier wagons. The further doors lead to an internal ramp, for cars to reach or leave the upper deck. Normally, the two decks load

and unload from opposite platforms simultaneously, so speeding up the operation. To span the space between doors and platforms, two bridging plates can be lowered from inside; these are operated by hydraulic rams concealed in the floor.

A small seating area for motorcyclists and their passengers is positioned over the vehicle entrance at the outer end of each loading/unloading wagon. The bikes travel securely housed under the ramp in a special cubicle, which accommodates three bikes in each wagon. A toilet is provided alongside the seating area. Spare wheelchairs for disabled people are also located inside the bike compartment.

Seating for motor-cyclists in double-deck loading wagon

Double-deck passenger-vehicle loading wagon

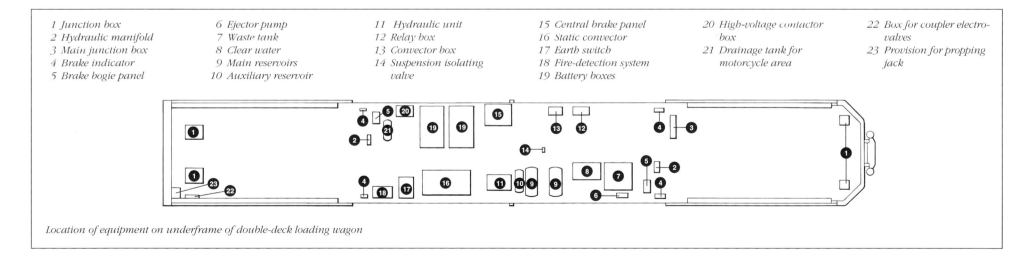

1 Junction box	6 Ejector pump	11 Hydraulic unit	15 Central brake panel	20 High-voltage contactor box	22 Box for coupler electro-valves
2 Hydraulic manifold	7 Waste tank	12 Relay box	16 Static convector	21 Drainage tank for	23 Provision for propping jack
3 Main junction box	8 Clear water	13 Convector box	17 Earth switch	motorcycle area	
4 Brake indicator	9 Main reservoirs	14 Suspension isolating	18 Fire-detection system		
5 Brake bogie panel	10 Auxiliary reservoir	valve	19 Battery boxes		

Location of equipment on underframe of double-deck loading wagon

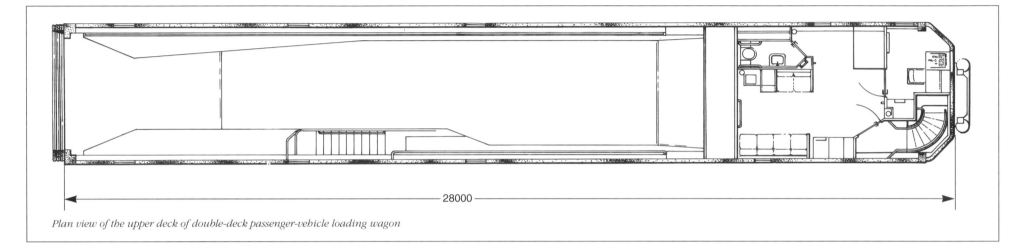

Plan view of the upper deck of double-deck passenger-vehicle loading wagon

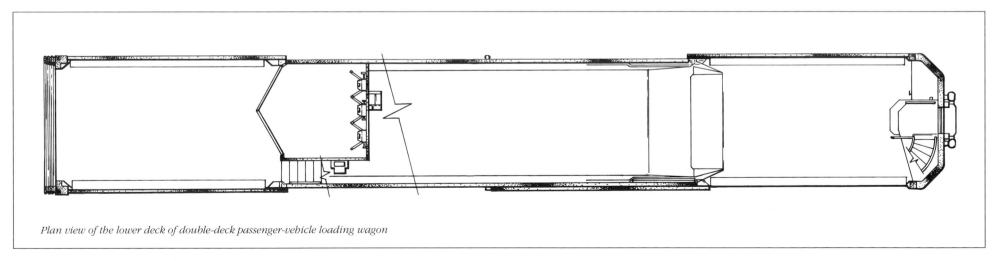

Plan view of the lower deck of double-deck passenger-vehicle loading wagon

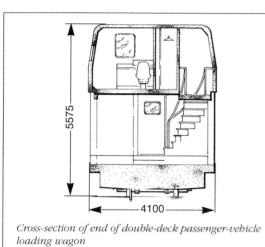

Cross-section of end of double-deck passenger-vehicle loading wagon

View inside double-deck loading wagon

Upper deck and internal stairs of double-deck loading wagon

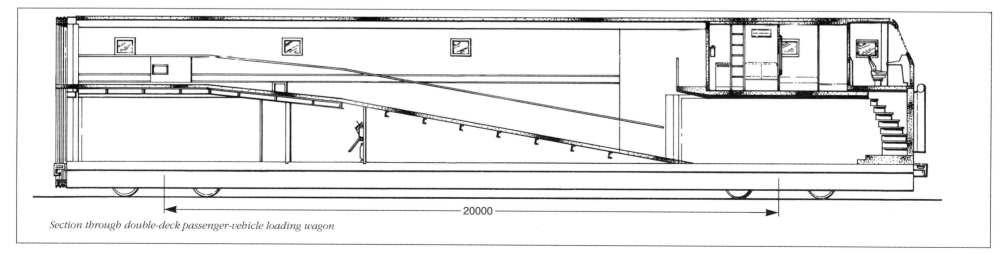

Section through double-deck passenger-vehicle loading wagon

A small driving cab positioned in the top left-hand corner of the outer end of the loading wagons is used for moving groups of carrier wagons in the stabling and maintenance areas. The cab, which is normally locked,

contains controls for low-speed driving and a panel for operating and monitoring the wagon's own systems, such as the loading doors; it is not fitted with a cab signalling system. For the same purpose a control box can also be connected outside the wagon to enable the maintenance staff to move a half-shuttle at a speed of no more than 33km/h. A spiral staircase alongside the cab connects the two decks.

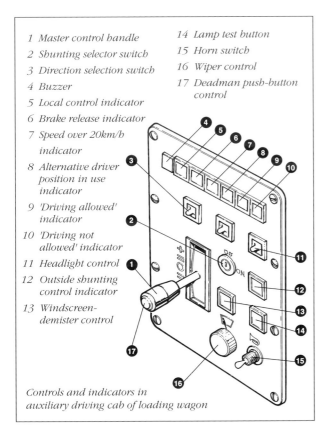

1 Master control handle
2 Shunting selector switch
3 Direction selection switch
4 Buzzer
5 Local control indicator
6 Brake release indicator
7 Speed over 20km/h indicator
8 Alternative driver position in use indicator
9 'Driving allowed' indicator
10 'Driving not allowed' indicator
11 Headlight control
12 Outside shunting control indicator
13 Windscreen-demister control
14 Lamp test button
15 Horn switch
16 Wiper control
17 Deadman push-button control

Controls and indicators in auxiliary driving cab of loading wagon

Auxiliary driving cab of double-deck loading wagon

Motorcycle storage area under ramp of double-deck loading wagon, with side door open (above) and closed (below)

Single-deck loading wagons

Single-deck shuttles require a more complex design of loading wagon capable of taking long and heavy vehicles.

The function of the single-deck loading wagon is to provide sufficient lateral space to allow a coach, or a car with a caravan, to align itself to drive through the rake of carrier wagons. The loading wagon does this by forming a bridge between each pair of terminal platforms. The bodywork, whose sole purpose is to link the carrier wagons with the toilets, consists of three hood canopies that telescope on to a fixed canopy at the outer end of the wagon during loading and unloading, so freeing three-quarters of the wagon's length for vehicles to manoeuvre. Long loading-plates on each side hinge down to bridge the gap between the wagon and the platform, thus allowing vehicles to use the entire width of the loading wagon and both platforms to align themselves. When every vehicle has loaded, the loading-plates are lifted and the canopies moved to enclose the entire floor area; seals between them are inflated to reduce the effects of pressure changes in the Tunnel. The canopies are moved by wire ropes and hydraulic motors; hand operation is also possible.

The greater width of vehicles using the SD shuttles means that there is no room for toilets in the carrier wagons. Instead, they are situated in an air-conditioned amenity area at the end of each loading wagon, behind a small driving cab, which is used in the same way as the cab in the DD loading wagon.

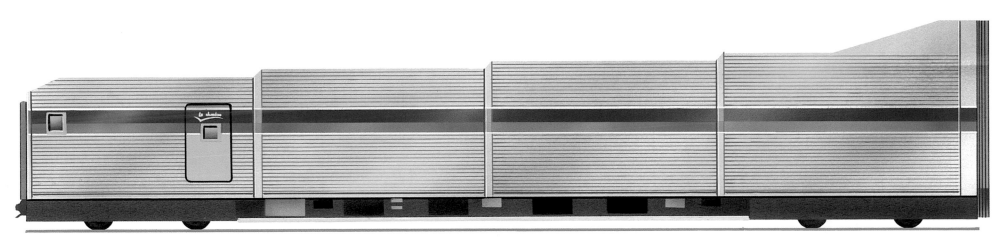

Single-deck passenger-vehicle loading wagon

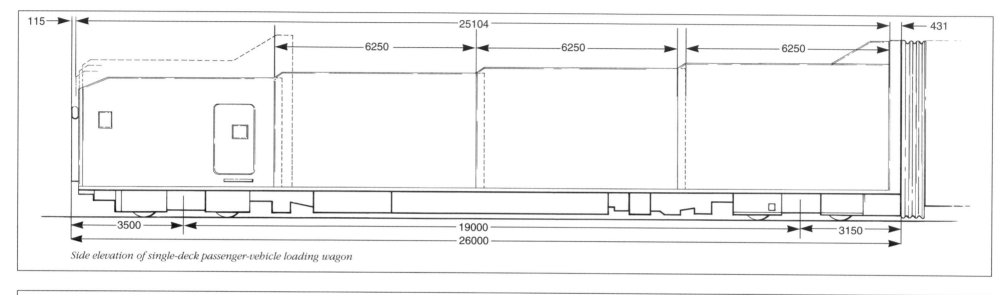

Side elevation of single-deck passenger-vehicle loading wagon

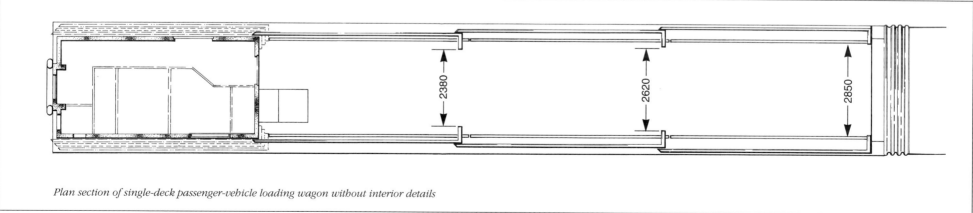

Plan section of single-deck passenger-vehicle loading wagon without interior details

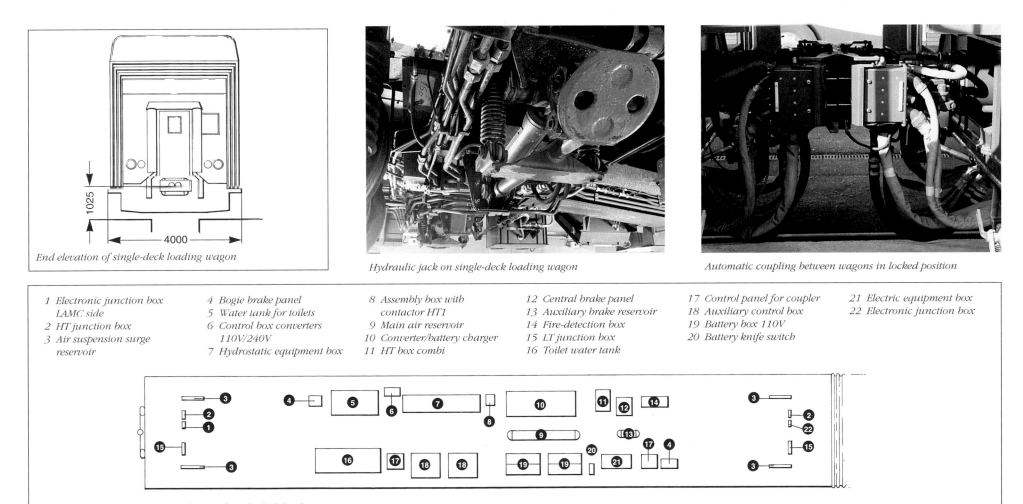

End elevation of single-deck loading wagon

Hydraulic jack on single-deck loading wagon

Automatic coupling between wagons in locked position

1 Electronic junction box
   LAMC side
2 HT junction box
3 Air suspension surge
   reservoir

4 Bogie brake panel
5 Water tank for toilets
6 Control box converters
   110V/240V
7 Hydrostatic equipment box

8 Assembly box with
   contactor HT1
9 Main air reservoir
10 Converter/battery charger
11 HT box combi

12 Central brake panel
13 Auxiliary brake reservoir
14 Fire-detection box
15 LT junction box
16 Toilet water tank

17 Control panel for coupler
18 Auxiliary control box
19 Battery box 110V
20 Battery knife switch

21 Electric equipment box
22 Electronic junction box

Location of equipment on underframe of single-deck loading wagon

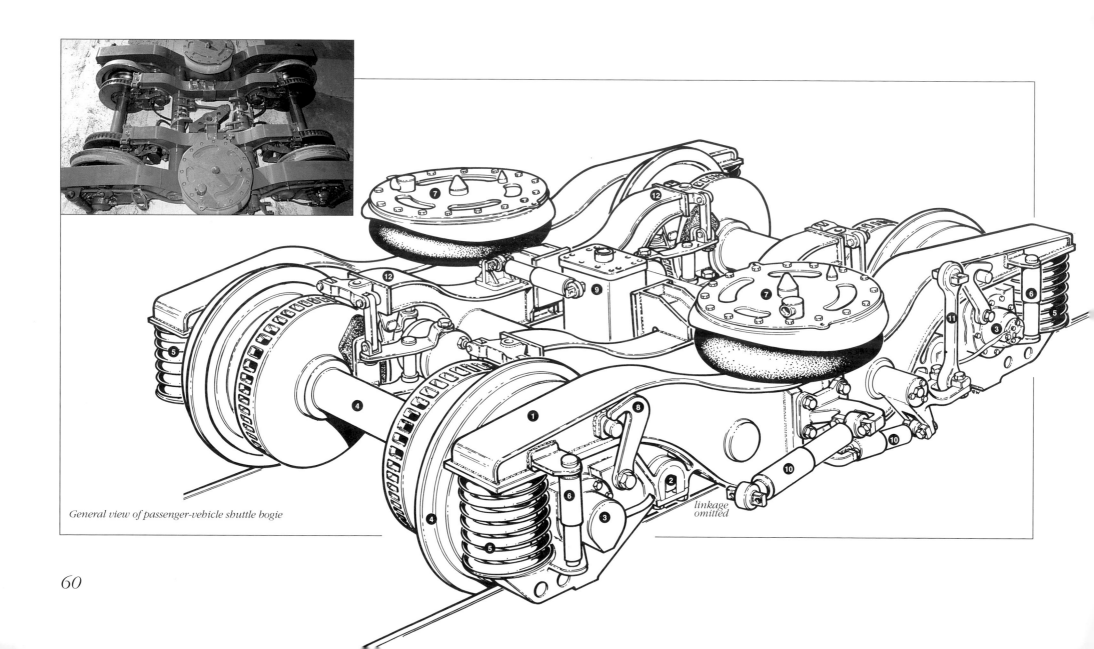

General view of passenger-vehicle shuttle bogie

linkage omitted

Bogies

The bogies must provide a satisfactory ride for passengers whether the wagon is fully loaded or nearly empty. They must also ensure that the wagon remains within the loading gauge at all times.

As shown in the diagram opposite, the bogie has a fabricated frame, H-shaped in plan (1). Under the upswept ends, pivots for the short radius-arms (2) support the axleboxes (3) for the wheel-sets (4). These rise and fall with 90mm vertical play to accommodate any irregularities in the track, and the coil springs (5) provide the primary suspension. Hydraulic dampers (6) are used to prevent any 'bounce'. The whole bogie is located on the underframe of the wagon by the central pivot and attached by the secondary suspension, which consists of two large air-bags (7). This arrangement is widely used on passenger rolling stock, including the latest TGV and Eurostar trains, although the empty/full weight changes on the Eurotunnel stock are far greater than those on conventional trains.

As well as giving the smoothest and quietest ride for passengers, the air-bags ensure that the bogie remains centred on curves. They also provide part of the restoring forces to keep it parallel with the vehicles. The air-bags are inflated from the train's compressed-air system, through a levelling valve actuated by the height of the body above the rail. Any change in the overall weight of the wagon causes it to rise or fall on its springs; the levelling valve will adjust the air pressure in the bags to restore the vehicle to its normal level. The primary suspension does not need any similar compensating device, as the top of the bogie frame remains between 812 and 815mm above rail level, whatever the load. Hooks (8), attached to the axleboxes, prevent the bogie frame rising too high in the unloaded condition, or when the wagons are jacked up for maintenance.

The pivot (9) is rigidly fixed to the underframe of the wagon, and a small amount of lateral play is permitted by the Z-linkage arrangement. To damp any oscillations and to prevent 'hunting' (rapid side-to-side angular motion) of the bogie at speed, two sets of hydraulic dampers (10) are provided between the bogie frame and the vehicle body. The high centre of gravity of a loaded wagon, especially the double-deck version, could lead to a roll developing when travelling. To prevent this, a torsion-bar passes through the bogie frame tubes, vertical links (11) connecting the cranks on its ends with the two sides of the body. Any attempt by the body to roll is thus opposed by the links twisting the ends of the torsion bar in opposite directions.

Four additional short arms (12) are attached to the cross-member of the bogie frame to support the braking equipment. (For clarity, this is not shown in the diagram, but the corresponding arrangements can be seen in the diagram of the freight shuttle bogie in chapter 3.) However, the brake discs on which the brake-pads engage can be seen, rigidly fixed to the axles between the wheels. On the passenger wagons the air-bag suspension pressure is also linked to the brake control system. Since the air pressure in the bags is related to the load of the vehicle, it is also used to vary the braking effort to match this load.

Air-conditioning

For several decades air-conditioning has been provided on high-quality railways throughout the world. This markedly improved the ambience of train travel, cooling the train in hot weather and reducing draughts and noise from outside, especially in tunnels. While air-conditioning is an important feature of the passenger-vehicle wagons, the system is required to perform another important and much more unusual function. This is to purge the wagons of fumes while vehicles are being loaded and unloaded, and so avoid passengers

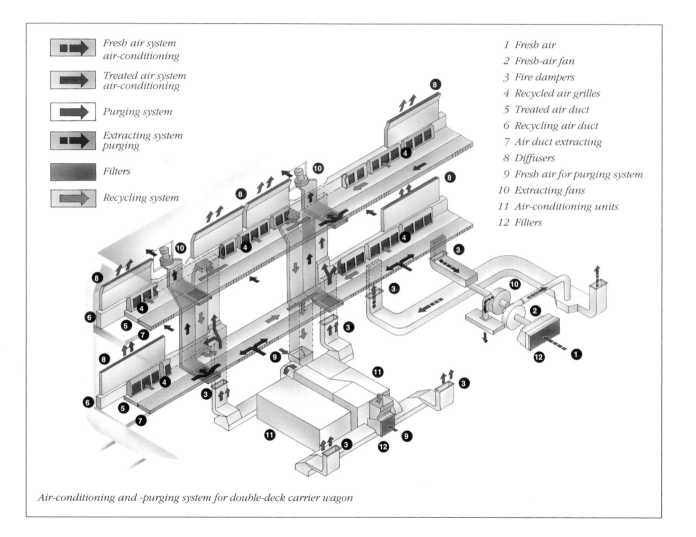

Fresh air system
air-conditioning

Treated air system
air-conditioning

Purging system

Extracting system
purging

Filters

Recycling system

1 Fresh air
2 Fresh-air fan
3 Fire dampers
4 Recycled air grilles
5 Treated air duct
6 Recycling air duct
7 Air duct extracting
8 Diffusers
9 Fresh air for purging system
10 Extracting fans
11 Air-conditioning units
12 Filters

Air-conditioning and -purging system for double-deck carrier wagon

having to endure an unpleasant atmosphere during the journey.

The diagram left illustrates the air-conditioning system on a DD carriage, the two separate car-decks making it more complex than the system on SD carriages. Two 2-tonne air-conditioning units (11) with a capacity of 60kW are fixed to the bottom of each wagon underframe. These heat or cool the air depending on outside conditions. The heating is done electrically using power from the locomotives, which is fed along the 1500V 'train line' running the length of the shuttle. The cooling units are powered from the same source via static converters in the 'A' wagons; they may require more energy during hot weather than the heaters consume in winter. The system is designed to keep the temperature in the passenger areas in the 'comfort envelope' of 18 to 20ºC (64 to 82ºF), even though the corresponding external temperatures vary from -5 to 38ºC (19 to 100ºF).

The treated air is circulated through ducts to lines of diffusers (8) along both inside walls of the wagons. Normally the air is extracted through grills (4) just above floor level, returning to the air-conditioning units to be recycled, except for approximately 15 per cent which is purged from the system by the underfloor fan. The main

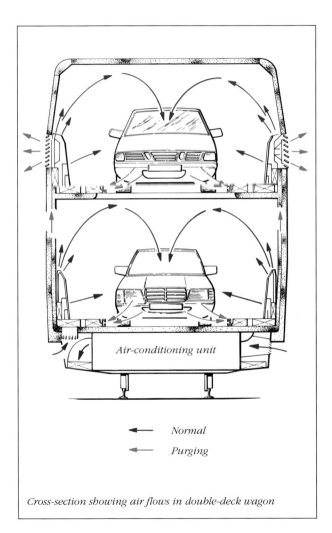

Air-conditioning unit

← *Normal*

← *Purging*

Cross-section showing air flows in double-deck wagon

fresh-air fan (2) makes up the displaced quantity, the air entering through filters. This system ensures that the noise level inside the carriages is no louder than that on high-speed passenger trains and that any pressure surges from the piston relief ducts (see chapter 8) will not cause discomfort. During a single trip, each passenger can be sure of receiving more than 8cu m of newly conditioned fresh air.

A further series of fans, each capable of handling 2500cu m per hour, is used to purge the wagon interiors during loading and unloading. Each double-deck wagon contains eight fans, each single-deck four. The fans pull the air from a series of ducts under the floors, with inlets positioned to catch the fumes from the vehicles before they spread around the wagon, and then exhaust it through grills positioned high on the outside of the wagons. The flow is sufficiently rapid to enable all the air inside the wagon to be changed once every 70 seconds. This is supplemented by fresh air blowing in through the loading doors when these are open. This purging system is operated manually, either by the train captain or locally.

This air-conditioning system requires no fewer than 38 electric motors on each wagon. Like every other system on the train, it is monitored by the train captain's equipment, which provides a warning if anything goes

wrong. Fire-dampers fitted at vital points throughout the ducting systems can be closed to stop the spread of fumes or smoke.

To provide power to this complex system, two 90kW units are provided under two of each 'triplet' of carriages. To ensure power if the train line is de-energised, batteries of 300Ah (amperes/hours) at 110v for the DD wagons and 250Ah for the SD wagons are provided in the underframe.

Communications

A complex audio and visual communications system enables the train captain to communicate with the passengers and crew as well as with the Control Centre (see chapter 13). After passengers joining a shuttle have stopped their vehicles, they will be briefed through the public information system, in both English and French, with safety and travel information. This is supplemented by text on the dot matrix screens in the ceiling ahead of them. During the 35-minute journey further announcements will be made and on arrival instructions are given to drive out of the shuttle. Throughout the journey it will also be possible to tune a car radio to a special frequency to receive information about the journey.

Responsibility for the safety and operation of the train rests with the train captain, and all the audio and visual messages to the passengers originate in the train captain's 'office' in the cab of the rear locomotive. Pre-recorded, routine information is transmitted by pressing the appropriate button or touch screen monitor. Special messages can be broadcast either to the whole train or to particular wagons. In addition, a special call system enables passengers to contact the train captain directly.

The train captain monitors the entire train primarily by means of a closed-circuit television system, with a camera at both ends of each wagon deck. All the images from a given wagon are presented simultaneously on a split-screen. In normal operating conditions each wagon is scanned in turn. However, the captain can 'home in' on a particular wagon at any time through a touch screen. In addition, if any sensor reports an important abnormal condition, the system automatically shows the wagon concerned; this largely relates to fire alarm and protection equipment.

All the other equipment on the shuttle is monitored by the train captain, who checks its performance. If an item of equipment, such as a fan in the air-conditioning system, were to stop, the captain's attention would immediately be drawn to it. Most equipment will re-set or reconfigure itself automatically to deal with this sort of eventuality. If human action is needed, this can be provided by the train captain, who can instruct the equipment to carry out the necessary action by calling up the system concerned on the monitor screens and pressing the appropriate button.

As described in chapter 1, the couplings between the wagons carry some 200 connectors for the circuits that run the length of the train carrying information to and from the train captain's office. Some of these circuits are dedicated to a particular function, while others are shared by a number of different systems. In all cases time-division multiplex redundant circuits are used. Each constantly scans the performance of all the functions involved, and receives the 'answers' to its electronic

Dot-matrix information board

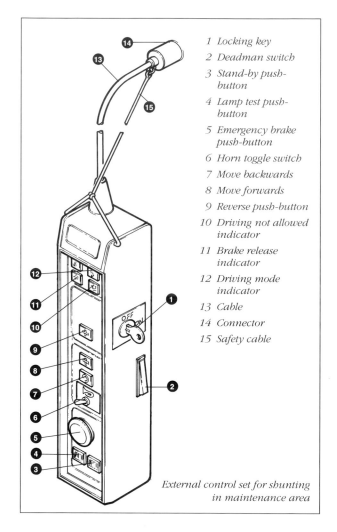

1 *Locking key*
2 *Deadman switch*
3 *Stand-by push-button*
4 *Lamp test push-button*
5 *Emergency brake push-button*
6 *Horn toggle switch*
7 *Move backwards*
8 *Move forwards*
9 *Reverse push-button*
10 *Driving not allowed indicator*
11 *Brake release indicator*
12 *Driving mode indicator*
13 *Cable*
14 *Connector*
15 *Safety cable*

External control set for shunting in maintenance area

'questions' a millisecond later.

At the front of the train, the driver operates the locomotives, obeying the commands of the signalling system (see chapter 11). The driver and train captain can discuss any unusual occurrence over the internal telephone system, and the train captain can also contact other crew members by radio-telephone. A radio voice-link to the train enables information to be passed to and from the Control Centre. Other pre-recorded or coded messages can also be transmitted directly.

The communications systems on the shuttles are thus extremely comprehensive, although only a small minority will be apparent to travellers. An impression of the scale of the equipment is, however, provided by the fact that each passenger-vehicle shuttle wagon contains over 50km of wiring, a considerable proportion of which is involved with communications.

High-capacity batteries are provided for stand-by purposes to power the communication circuits.

External control set in use for moving half-train in maintenance area

Scharfenberg coupling on a passenger-vehicle loading wagon

Passenger/crew contact-point

Fire-prevention

The shuttle wagons are equiped with a comprehensive fire-detection and extinguishing system. Each wagon contains passenger-operated alarms as well as a series of detectors that are automatically triggered by smoke, fumes and inflammable vapours. These detectors are sensitive to ions, or ultra-violet radiations, smoke and gases, and are located in the ceiling, walls and floor or drainage duct of each wagon.

Even though smoking is not permitted anywhere on the shuttle, it is important to avoid false alarms that could cause unnecessary action by the train crew or concern to the passengers. For this reason, two ordinary detectors or one passenger-operated alarm have to operate before the system registers a 'Level 1 Alarm'. This alerts the train captain in the rear locomotive as well as the train crew, who will immediately go to the wagon concerned to investigate and deal with the situation. The wagon's air-conditioning system is also automatically shut down and its air-duct fire-dampers are closed.

Two hand-operated portable extinguishers in each wagon can be used to deal with a small fire. If the smoke density increases further, the sensors set off a 'Level 2 Alarm', which causes the public address system to instruct passengers to evacuate the wagon concerned. Guided by the crew, they will enter the adjacent wagons through the end pass-doors. If the problem occurs in the part of the shuttle occupied by disabled passengers, they will be given special assistance.

If the smoke density continues to increase, a 'Level 3 Alarm' is triggered; this automatically discharges Halon gas into the area concerned. This is a very effective means of putting a fire out, and similar equipment is provided in many computer rooms throughout the world. If necessary, crew members can make a second manual Halon discharge, since each wagon has substantial reserves. Once everyone has been safely evacuated, the crew can use breathing apparatus to search the affected wagon for the cause of the fire.

Sensors also detect fuel leaking from a vehicle on to the wagon floor, and trigger a discharge of water with foaming agent to flush it into a sump below floor level. The sump has its own fire-extinguishing system, and is automatically emptied when the shuttle reaches the terminal maintenance and washing area.

Hand-operated fire-extinguisher on interior wall of carrier wagon

Emergency door on a passenger-vehicle wagon

The Freight Shuttle Fleet

Each freight shuttle is formed of two separate halves, or rakes. Each half contains one loading and one unloading wagon and 14 carrier wagons. There is a locomotive at both ends, with a club car behind the leading one.

Eurotunnel's initial order was for eight shuttles. The total fleet is therefore:

33 loading/unloading wagons, including one spare

228 carrier wagons, including four spares

9 club cars, including one spare

Wagon design

Under the terms of Eurotunnel's concession (see Introduction), the freight shuttle wagons have to be capable of carrying 44-tonne lorries. Constructing a railway wagon to fulfil this requirement while remaining within the 22-tonne axle-load limit imposed by the track presented the designers with a difficult task. A closed design, like that of the passenger-vehicle shuttle carriages, would have added considerably to the weight, and there was no justification in providing full passenger

comfort and safety to enable a relatively small number of drivers to travel through the Tunnel in the cabs of their lorries.

Accordingly, Eurotunnel decided to carry lorries in semi-open wagons with drivers travelling in a club car at the front of the train, where they can rest away from their vehicles. Separating drivers from their vehicles did away with the need for air-conditioning and many communication systems, as well as for end doors on the wagons. The semi-open design prevents anything that

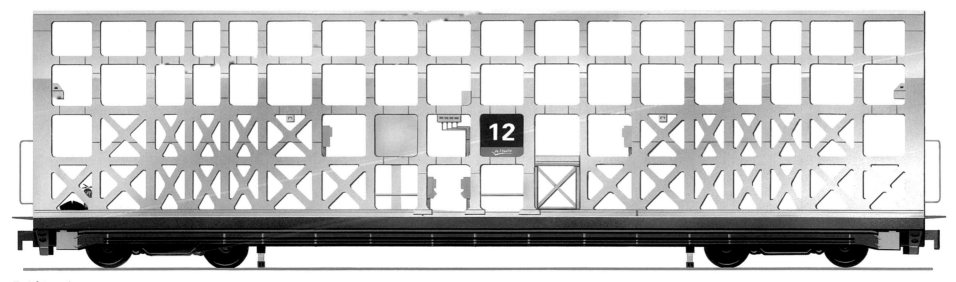

Freight carrier wagon

The body of a freight carrier wagon being delivered

might work loose on a lorry blowing about and causing the catenary to arc, or damaging lineside equipment.

The wagon structure is a trellis of stainless steel, assembled by standard production techniques and spot-welded. The design is most unusual, with diagonal members positioned where the structure is most stressed. This arrangement provides a more efficient structure than an open flat-wagon design. As on the passenger-vehicle wagons, overlapping horizontal plates provide a bridge

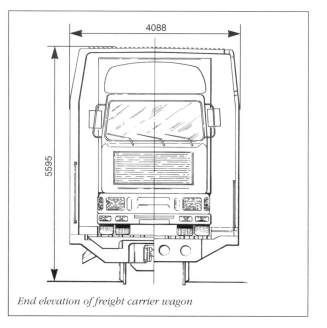

End elevation of freight carrier wagon

between wagons, but the ends are otherwise entirely open.

Drivers, their passengers and Le Shuttle staff enter and leave the wagon through a door-sized opening on each side. When loading is complete, a bus picks up drivers and any passengers and drives them along the platform to the club car marshalled at the front of the shuttle, just behind the locomotive.

Each freight shuttle consists of two identical halves, or rakes, each of which is made up of 14 carrier wagons, semi-permanently coupled, and a loading and an unloading wagon. The total length of the shuttle, including two locomotives and the club car, is 730m. This is just 46m shorter than the passenger shuttle; the same platforms can therefore be used for both types of shuttle.

Lorries enter the shuttle via the loading wagon, and then drive through the carrier wagons until signalled to stop; side kerbs, 150 mm high, acting as guides. Although protection arms (see chapter 2) are not installed, each lorry is carefully positioned so as to balance its weight between the wagon's two bogies, and is chocked to prevent it moving. A sunken section with drainage facilities runs along the centre of the wagon floor to collect any leaking oil etc; this is automatically emptied during washing and maintenance. Overhead lighting is provided, and an interior control panel

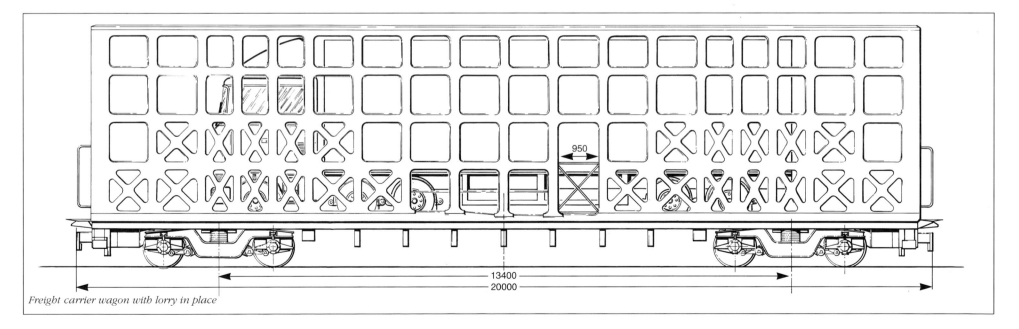

Freight carrier wagon with lorry in place

enables staff to monitor equipment mounted on the underframe.

The electrical system of the wagons is relatively simple. Supplies at 400V three-phase ac and 110V dc provide power for lighting, jacks and bridging-plate operation and for the lorry plug-in system. Lorries with temperature control or refrigeration equipment can plug into the two electrical supply points (400V ac or 110V dc) provided on each wagon side, since the diesel motor that acts as the normal power source for these purposes must be shut down during the journey.

Stabilising beams are provided on the carrier wagons, and stabilising jacks on the loading/unloading wagons, to prevent deflections in the suspension system and maintain complete stability during loading and unloading (see also chapter 2).

BREDA-FIAT was responsible for manufacturing the freight shuttles, and the bogies were constructed by FIAT Ferroviaria at its Savigliano works near Turin, Italy.

In theory a fire could break out in a lorry travelling on the shuttle, just as it could in a car on one of the passenger-vehicle shuttles. On the latter, passengers or train crew would raise the alarm; in addition the closed shuttle wagons are fitted with automatic fire-detection sensors (see chapter 2). The semi-open construction of

Unloading a lorry on the Calais Terminal

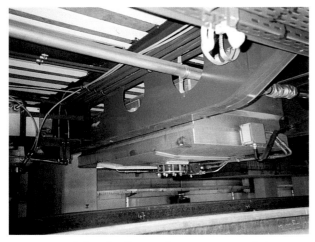

Drainage tank for oil spillage under carrier wagon deck

Power point for refrigerated lorries

the freight wagons means that effective fire-detection equipment cannot be fitted. Instead detectors have been installed on the loading wagons. These are supplemented by additional detectors placed at intervals along the Tunnel, behind closed doors in the cross-passages where they can easily be maintained by staff working from the service tunnel. Small fans continuously suck a stream of air from the tunnels into each detector where it is tested for fumes and smoke.

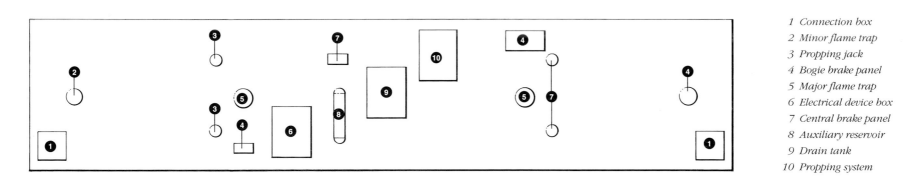

Underfloor system location plan on freight carrier wagon

1 Connection box
2 Minor flame trap
3 Propping jack
4 Bogie brake panel
5 Major flame trap
6 Electrical device box
7 Central brake panel
8 Auxiliary reservoir
9 Drain tank
10 Propping system

Loading/unloading wagons

The size and weight of lorries make loading and unloading a much more complicated operation than loading cars. Manoeuvring space is required to align an articulated vehicle, or a lorry and trailer, so that it can drive through the train of carrier wagons. Although at first sight the freight loading wagons appear to be simple low-sided wagons, sophisticated features have been incorporated to cope with heavy and moving loads.

The wagon's sides are in fact bridging-plates which, during loading and unloading, are lowered by concealed hydraulic jacks (to the accompaniment of warning 'bleeps') to cover the gap between the floor of the wagon and the platforms on both sides. Stabilising jacks are also lowered on to longitudinal beams beside the tracks to ensure stability during loading (see page 70). In this way the wagon is converted into a solid bridge between the platforms for a length of over 23m; interlocks ensure that all the props are retracted before the shuttle departs.

With the bridging plates lowered, a lorry can then use the full width of both platforms, plus that of the wagon itself, to align its trailer or semi-trailer with the first carrier wagon. When the shuttle is ready to depart, the plates are raised to come within the loading gauge. This operation is controlled by the train captain from his cabin in the club car.

During remarshalling in the terminals, a half-shuttle sometimes has to be propelled for some distance with the loading wagon leading. With the locomotive some 400m away, this would be difficult even at slow speeds, and so a set of shunting controls is provided in the cabin at the end of the wagon.

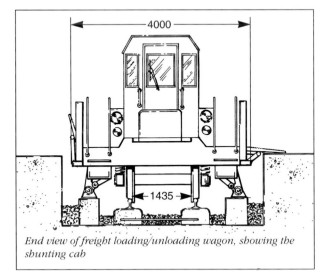

End view of freight loading/unloading wagon, showing the shunting cab

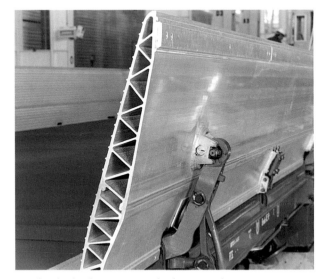

Loading/unloading wagon, side plates raised

Bridging plate between wagons

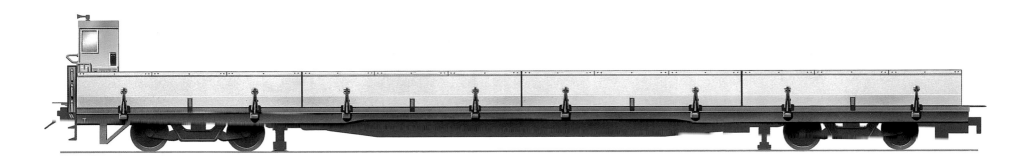

Freight loading/unloading wagon

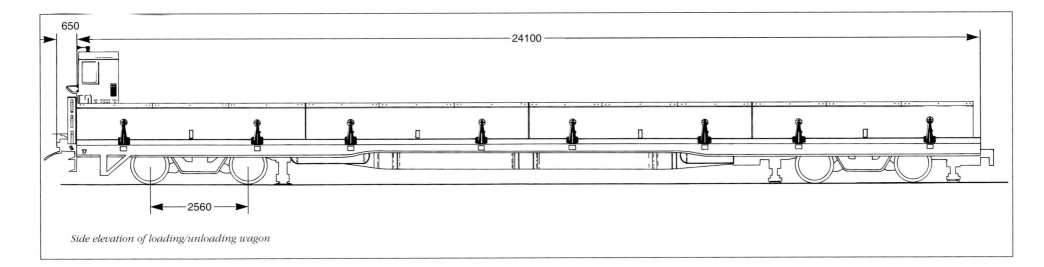

Side elevation of loading/unloading wagon

650

24100

2560

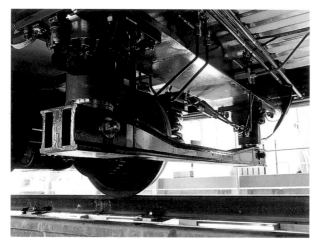

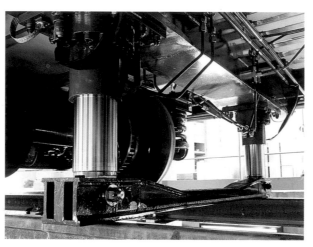

Freight carrier wagon stabilising jacks, retracted

Freight carrier wagon stabilising jacks, lowered

End jacking-pad on loading wagon in the lowered position

1 Central brake control unit box assembly
2 Brake control unit box assembly
3 Air reservoir pneumatic system assembly
4 Static converter – inverter assembly

5 Static converter assembly
6 Battery charger assembly
7 Hydrostatic power unit assembly
8 Assembly batteries box
9 Assembly box HT1
10 Central propping mechanism

11 Electric equipment box
12 Electric equipment box (relay)
13 Battery switch box assembly
14 Relay box
15 Carrier side HT junction box
16 Carrier side LT junction box

17 Carrier side 400V junction box
18 Carrier side electronic junction box
19 Semi-permanent coupler carrier side
20 Automatic coupler locomotive side

21 Locomotive side HT junction box
22 End propping mechanism
23 Locomotive side electronic junction box
24 High-voltage sensor box
25 Locomotive side LT junction box

26 Locomotive side flexible control layout
27 Carrier side flexible control layout
28 Hydrostatic system
29 Auxiliary relay box assembly

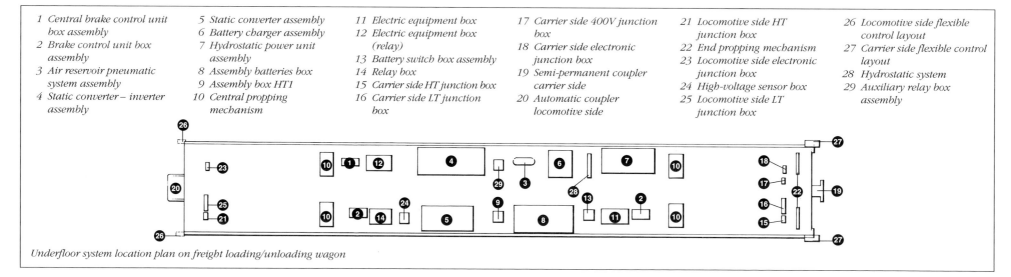

Underfloor system location plan on freight loading/unloading wagon

View along the track in platform area showing walls for stabilising jacks

Shunting cabin at outer end of loading/unloading wagon

Bogies

The bogies used on the loading wagons are the same as those on the carrier wagons. Because the loading wagons always operate empty, their bogies are not fitted with load-sensors to control the braking forces. The heavy axle-loading and different suspension characteristics of the freight shuttle wagons led the builder, FIAT, to propose a lighter and cheaper bogie than that used in the passenger-vehicle shuttle wagons, although its design is similar.

As shown in the diagram right, the main frame consists of an H-shaped welded fabrication (1), with four shorter arms (2) attached to the cross-member (3). These support the brake gear (4), which is hung from their ends. The two wheel-sets (5) are guided and attached to the main fabrication by short radial arms which link the roller-bearing axleboxes for all longitudinal forces. To support the greater weight, twin helical springs (6) are located vertically between the bogie frame and the roller-bearing support, which forms the primary suspension on each side of the axleboxes (7). The outer springs have hydraulic dampers mounted inside them (8). The 'rail-shaped' pieces of steel (9) attached to the top of each axlebox normally slide loosely between guides on the main frame, and form 'stops' to limit the

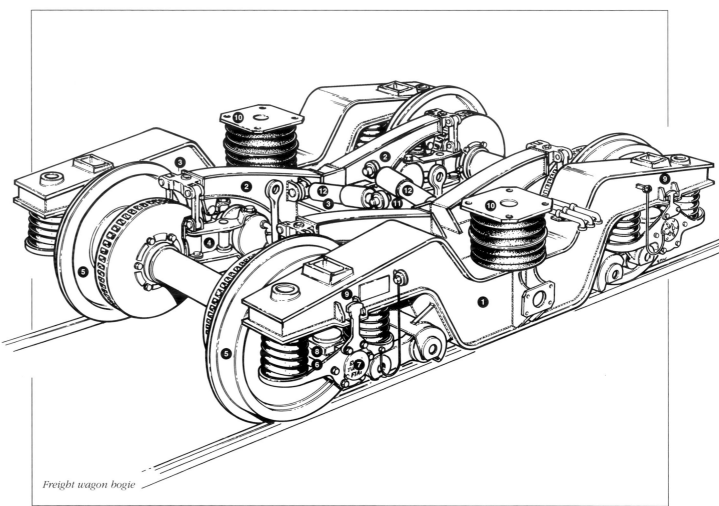

Freight wagon bogie

vertical movement of the axle and permit the wagon and bogie to be lifted without losing the axles.

The secondary suspension is provided by a pair of hard rubber springs (10) forming the side links between the bogie frame and the vehicle. They are limited to a 32mm vertical excursion. Bolted at their tops to the wagon underframe, they enable the bogie to rotate about the drawgear pivot (11 omitted for clarity) on curves, and also provide some of the restoring forces to keep it parallel with the vehicle's underframe on straight stretches of the track. They also act as noise dampers. Hydraulic dampers (12) horizontally mounted between the bogie and the underframe prevent the bogie 'hunting' at higher speeds.

The rubber springs and the central drawgear transmit the traction and braking forces between the bogie and

the vehicle body. The drawgear is rigidly fixed to the underframe, and fits into the central slot in the bogie cross-member. The pivot deals only with the rotational movements, since the other forces between the bogie and wagon body are handled by different parts of the equipment.

As on other shuttle bogies, the brakes are air-operated electrically. The air cylinders move the ends of the callipers outwards, forcing the four brake-pads into contact with both sides of the larger-diameter discs (13) rigidly fixed to the axles. As is usual in railway practice, the discs are hollow, with integrally cast spacers between the two faces. At speed these act as fans, providing a flow of cooling air. Because the weight of any freight wagon varies widely (between 36 and 80

tonnes) depending on whether or not it is loaded, load-sensors and microprocessor controls regulate the braking forces, and anti-wheel-slide electronic-speed control devices are fitted.

Club Cars

Lorry drivers and their passengers travel in their own club car, or amenity coach, marshalled just behind the front locomotive. An up-market design was selected, based on the first class passenger coaches used in the Italian State Railways' ETR 500 electric train-sets, which reach 270km/h on the 'Direttissima' high-speed lines. However, because such speeds will not be attained in the Tunnel it has been possible to use a simpler bogie. The bogie chosen has been used extensively on other

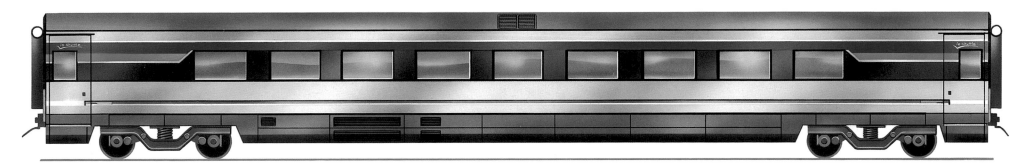

Club car

Interior of club car

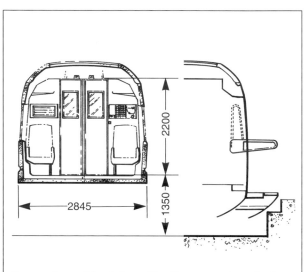

Cross-sections of the club car. The diagram on the right shows the positioning of the footsteps for use in the terminals

continental main-line rolling-stock operating at speeds of up to 160km/h, and is basically the same design as that used on the freight wagons, but with softer springing.

A number of other changes have also been made to the basic vehicle to adapt it to its new role. Inside a section has been closed off to provide space for the train captain and the control equipment, while another area has been provided to accommodate a catering trolley. Because the club car is built to the standard UIC loading

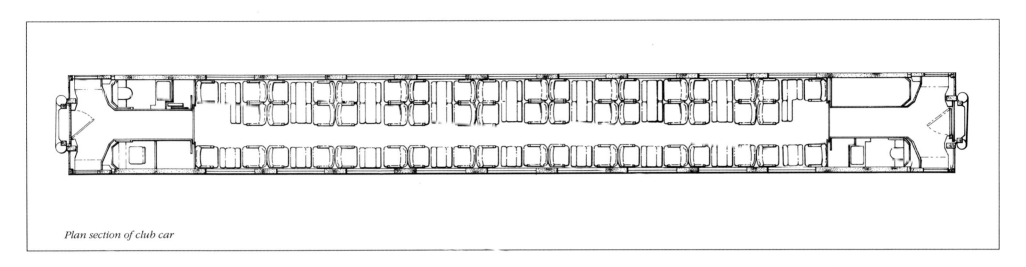

Plan section of club car

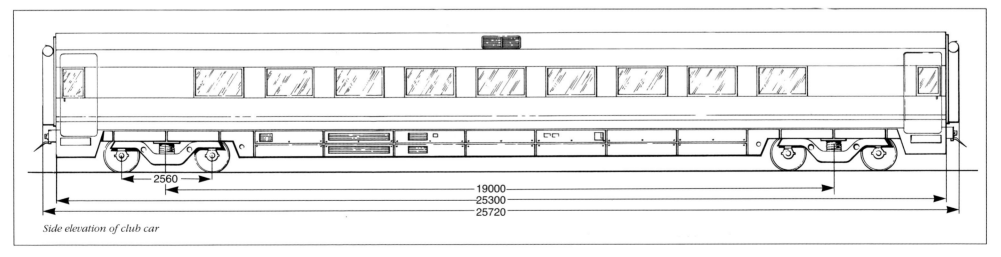

2560

19000
25300
25720

Side elevation of club car

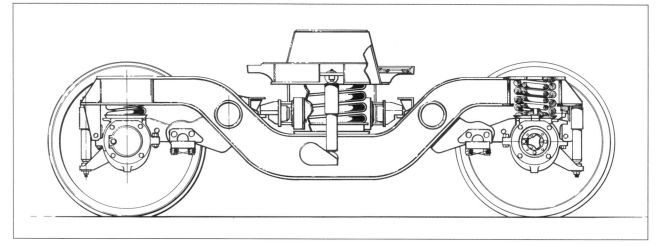

Above and below, club car bogie

Train captain's control panel cabin in club car

gauge, it is much narrower than the other shuttle rolling-stock, although the same width as the locomotives. The resulting gap between the car and the terminal platform (and the tunnel walkways if a train has to be evacuated) is bridged by a retractable flap, 670mm wide, that slides out below the foot-steps provided at each doorway; a hand-rail also swings down from the end of the vehicle to provide assistance.

Each club car has seating for 52 passengers, arranged in pairs on one side of the off-set aisle and in groups of four on the other. Tables with folding flaps are provided for each bay of seats. The coach is air-conditioned;

window blinds are supplied for passengers who find the contrast too great as they emerge from the Tunnel. Toilets and a public address system are also provided.

One feature of the Italian ETR 500 trains that has been retained in the club car is the continuous dark band of glazing along its length, although the actual windows are conventionally situated by each bay of seats. This is now a common design feature on railway stock; a similar effect was achieved by painting the upper panels of BR's InterCity stock dark grey to avoid the windows breaking up the line of the coaches. All the vehicles in the train thus blend visually into a whole.

Although Eurotunnel's initial rolling stock fleet consists of no less than 567 vehicles, when made up into trains these form only nine passenger-vehicle shuttles and eight freight shuttles. Each shuttle represents over 10 per cent of its type: a significant proportion of the assets with which Eurotunnel has to provide a service 24 hours a day, 52 weeks a year. Regular preventative inspection, servicing and overhaul, in particular of the safety systems, are thus crucial to efficient operations.

Both routine maintenance and major overhauls of all rolling stock will be carried out within the system. The principal servicing area and workshop are situated on the Calais Terminal, with subsidiary facilities at Folkestone (see below). While the size of the shuttle wagons makes them 'captive' to Eurotunnel's system, the locomotives are small enough to run over some continental main lines, so that heavy overhauls can, if necessary, take place at any suitable workshop.

Each locomotive and its allocated rake (half-shuttle) of wagons are inspected and serviced at weekly intervals. On other railways, locomotive running-gear is normally inspected at intervals of between six and thirty-seven days. Intensive utilisation and high axle-loadings are among the factors that led Eurotunnel to adopt its initial seven-day system. Even so, the locomotives can average some 5000km between each inspection. While wagons would normally be serviced after 10,000km, it is clearly more efficient and practicable to keep locomotives and their wagons together.

Regular servicing and maintenance are essential for the efficient operation of Le Shuttle. Here a freight shuttle under commission, passes through one of the crossovers, which themselves are major elements of the Tunnel's electromechanical infrastructure requiring regular maintenance

Each type of specialised equipment on the wagons has its own inspection, servicing and maintenance intervals, with work timetabled to coincide with the regular weekly inspections. Maintenance intervals for such equipment are based on distance, or time in service, or calendar date depending on the most efficient

Raised platforms facilitate maintenance inspection

arrangement for each item. A computer system automatically tells maintenance staff what requires doing, and when. Planning takes into account the varying seasonal demands on the shuttles' capacity.

Each weekly maintenance check takes about eight hours for a passenger shuttle, and about six for a freight shuttle, as these are less complex. Any piece of equipment that cannot be checked and overhauled during the weekly visit is replaced, thus giving more time for the work to be carried out, if necessary by a specialist contractor. Even a bogie can be changed in less than one hour. Although rolling stock maintenance is carried out 24 hours per day, more of the work takes place at night because traffic is less at that time.

Trouble-shooting

Well-planned preventative servicing and maintenance provide the key to efficient operations. Nevertheless, minor faults and breakdowns are inevitable. A team of 'trouble-shooters' is based on the platforms at each terminal, equipped to undertake small running repairs during unloading and loading. The train captain reports any faults to the Control Centre, in transit if necessary, and this advance information enables the team to plan the necessary action before the shuttle reaches the

terminal. Safety considerations are paramount in the decision to allow a locomotive or wagon to continue in service.

The maintenance depots

The principal servicing depot is situated on the Calais Terminal. The main facility has a floor area of 10,000sq m, and is divided into 'servicing' and 'workshop' sections by the internal offices and stores. Four tracks, each equipped with electric contact wire, run through the building in the servicing area. These are used for the routine weekly visit by each rake of wagons and locomotive: the rake moves progressively through the building, three wagons at a time, controlled by radio from the floor alongside. These routine examinations are supplemented by some annual preventative maintenance work, the whole programme being planned to even out the workload and minimise the time each rake is out of service. Only when major work is necessary is an individual wagon or triplet taken out of a rake and moved into the workshop area for attention.

As shown in the cross-section diagram on page 85, there are access platforms at floor and roof level, although the latter can only be used after the catenary has been isolated. Under the same conditions a small crane can lift items off the roof or out of the interior of a locomotive. In addition, fork-lift trucks run under the platforms and tracks to convey heavy items of underfloor equipment. Some of these are also rather large, and on three tracks sections of rail can be swung sideways to improve access. The fourth track is equipped with a Hegenscheidt wheel-lathe, which re-profiles wagon and locomotive tyres without the bogie having to be removed, and is equipped with its own hauling system. A pit with moveable sections of track and a traverser permits the removal and care of complete bogies from a wagon on any of the four tracks.

Servicing a wagon bogie from the pit

Aerial view of the maintenance depot on the Calais Terminal, with loading platforms in background

The workshop also has four tracks, but without catenary. One track is mounted on pillars to facilitate work on underfloor equipment. The other three tracks are laid at floor level, with pits between the rails, and are serviced by a 25-tonne overhead crane. A second overhead crane, capable of lifting 10 tonnes, serves one of the tracks and also covers the area where various machine tools are situated. One track is also equipped with twelve 17.5-tonne jacks, which can raise a complete triplet off the rails without uncoupling the individual wagons. On another track a set of four 35-tonne jacks can lift a locomotive off its bogies. A series of small turntables leads to special tracks on which the bogies can be moved around the workshop.

The smaller servicing facilities at the Folkestone Terminal supplement those at Calais and also carry out emergency repairs. There are two adjoining buildings. A small workshop with a floor area of 750sq m contains a single track equipped with a pit and four 35-tonne jacks which can lift any shuttle wagon or locomotive off the rails. There is no catenary in this shop, which is also used to overhaul the diesel-electric locomotive fleet and Eurotunnel road vehicles.

The second shed, 115m long, is provided with overhead power lines. It is connected at both ends with the terminal loop lines, so enabling shuttles to enter, receive attention and then return to service. The track is

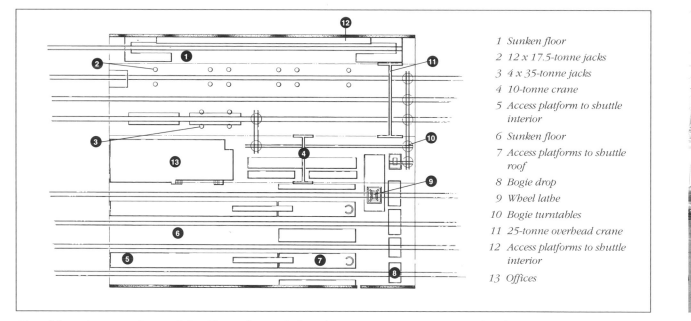

1 Sunken floor
2 12 x 17.5-tonne jacks
3 4 x 35-tonne jacks
4 10-tonne crane
5 Access platform to shuttle interior
6 Sunken floor
7 Access platforms to shuttle roof
8 Bogie drop
9 Wheel lathe
10 Bogie turntables
11 25-tonne overhead crane
12 Access platforms to shuttle interior
13 Offices

Plan of the maintenance depot at Calais. The top four tracks form the maintenance area; servicing takes place on the lower four tracks

Shuttle locomotive and single-deck loading wagon on the track above the sunken floor in the Calais maintenance depot

mounted on pillars 1m above the sunken floor to facilitate access to the equipment on the wagon underframes. Platforms enable staff to reach the wagon interiors and roofs; access to the latter is prevented until the catenary has been isolated.

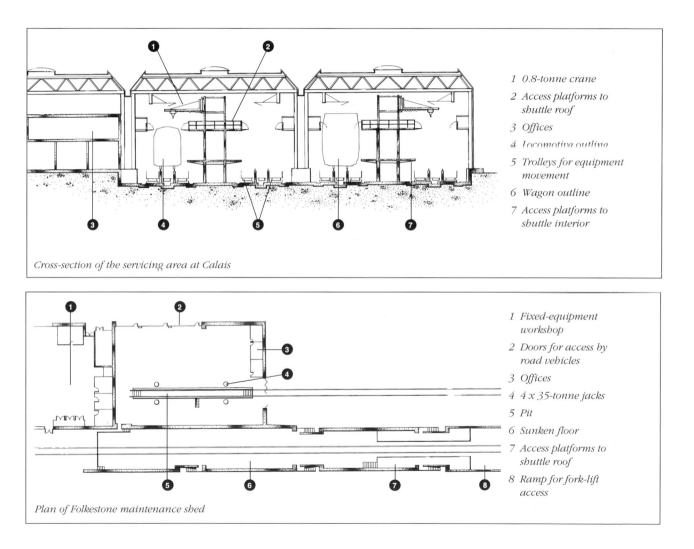

Cross-section of the servicing area at Calais

1 0.8-tonne crane
2 Access platforms to shuttle roof
3 Offices
4 Locomotive outline
5 Trolleys for equipment movement
6 Wagon outline
7 Access platforms to shuttle interior

Plan of Folkestone maintenance shed

1 Fixed-equipment workshop
2 Doors for access by road vehicles
3 Offices
4 4 x 35-tonne jacks
5 Pit
6 Sunken floor
7 Access platforms to shuttle roof
8 Ramp for fork-lift access

Freight shuttle wagons inside the Calais servicing area

The maintenance shed and fixed-equipment workshop on the Folkestone Terminal

Staffing

There are about 160 maintenance staff, together with about a further 100 employed by various sub-contractors. The majority is based at Calais; only 15 are normally allocated to Folkestone. However, if extra staff are suddenly required at one terminal, it is only 35 minutes away by shuttle.

Interior of Folkestone maintenance shed showing the roof access platforms and ramp leading to the sunken floor

Locomotives

On any electrified railway it is necessary to provide alternative traction to haul trains when the supply system has to be isolated for maintenance or safety purposes. It was thus clear from an early stage of the Channel Tunnel project that a second form of motive power would be needed for such occasions, as well as for rescuing any train that had broken down. On some tunnel systems, such as the Paris Metro and London Underground, battery-electric locomotives are used. However, these are heavy, and their range on a single battery charge is too short for a system the size of the Channel Tunnel; nor would they have had the capacity to rescue a stalled shuttle train. This requires a power of at least 1500kW (2000hp) and a minimum of six axles to provide the necessary adhesion to cope with the steep gradients.

The decision was therefore taken to obtain diesel-electric locomotives for this purpose, but ones that did not produce too many pollutants and were not noisy. Sufficient power would be required to haul 300-tonne engineers' trains at 80km/h, as well as to move a 2600-tonne shuttle, complete with its own 'dead' electric locomotives, up the 1 in 90 gradient at 50km/h. Studies showed that it would be preferable to use single locomotives for maintenance trains but twin locomotives, operating in multiple, for rescue, thus providing eight axles for adhesion.

As only five locomotives were required, a purpose-built design would have been too expensive. So, from the choices available, a variant of the 120 Class 6400 Bo-Bo locomotives employed on Netherlands Railways (*Nederlandse Spoorwegen* – NS) was selected. Built at Kiel, Germany, by Krupp/MaK and ASEA Brown Boveri

The Eurotunnel DE6400 diesel-electric servicing and rescue locomotive

(ABB), these entered service on NS from 1987. The Eurotunnel locomotives are known as DE6400, but are numbered 0001 to 0005.

A number of changes were made to the original design to meet Eurotunnel's requirements. The main diesel motor was de-rated from 1180 to 940kW (1580 to 1280hp) at 40°C, or 1040kW under atmospheric conditions of up to 38°C, and 1 Bar pressure. This reduction is to compensate for the back-pressure required to force the exhaust through the special scrubber unit (see pages 93-4).

As on the original NS version, a small auxiliary diesel-electric motor is also fitted to provide power when the

Class 6400 locomotives in operation in the Netherlands (above) and the Eurotunnel variants under construction at Kiel

main motor is shut down. One of its duties is to keep the water in the cooling system at an operating temperature of about 40°C, so that the main motor will start quickly without emitting fumes.

A full TVM 430 cab-signalling system (see chapter 11) is installed to enable the locomotives to operate in the Tunnel.

Body

The body of the locomotive is constructed on a rigid underframe, 50cm deep throughout, with reinforced ends. A single raised cab enables the driver to look in each direction over the two 'bonnets' of different lengths, which contain the main equipment. The longer (rear) one houses the two diesel-electric sets and their related auxiliaries, including the cooling system. Behind the cab are housed the rectifiers and inverters that provide the variable-frequency three-phase supply to the traction motors, as well as the signalling and brake equipment. The batteries and their charger are slung below the underframe between the bogies, together with the 3500-litre fuel tank and compressed-air reservoirs.

In service, the locomotives must be able to couple with several different types of vehicles. On maintenance trains they must haul wagons fitted with standard UIC screw couplings with centres 1050mm above rail level. In maintenance or rescue work, they also couple on to the front of shuttle locomotives in the same way. When rescuing part of a failed train, however, they must engage with the automatic Scharfenberg couplers at the lower height of 680mm. As a consequence the locomotives' buffer-beams are quite complex, with three coupling devices at two different heights.

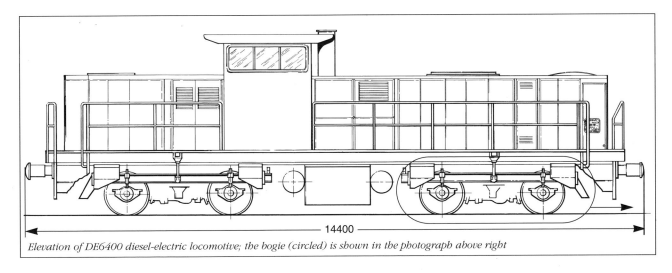

Elevation of DE6400 diesel-electric locomotive; the bogie (circled) is shown in the photograph above right

14400

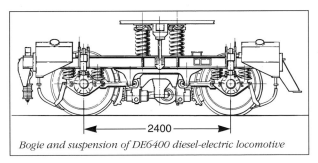

2400

Bogie and suspension of DE6400 diesel-electric locomotive

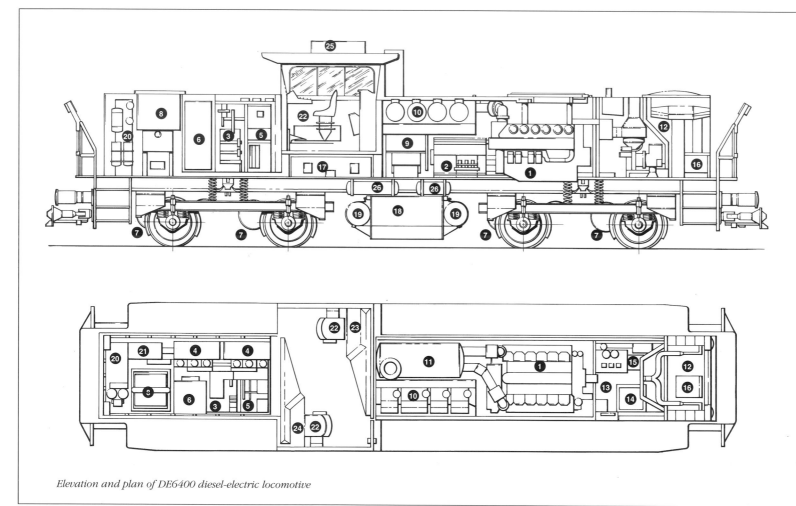

1 Diesel engine
2 Main generator
3 Rectifier
4 Inverter
5 Apparatus rack
6 Electronics cabinet
7 Traction motor
8 Brake resistor
9 Traction motor fan
10 Combustion air inlet
11 Exhaust silencer and catalyst
12 Cooling equipment
13 Hydrostatic pump
14 Air compressor
15 Auxiliary diesel generator set
16 Auxiliary battery casing
17 Main battery casing
18 Fuel tank
19 Main air reservoir
20 Brake panel
21 ATP cabinet
22 Driver's seat
23 Main driver's desk
24 Auxiliary driver's desk
25 Air conditioning
26 Compressed air reservoir

Elevation and plan of DE6400 diesel-electric locomotive

The two twin-axle bogies are mounted under the ends of the body. The axles have horizontal traction-links, and a hard-rubber cone inside the twin helical springs of each axlebox's primary suspension provides lateral restraint. There are hydraulic dampers between the axleboxes and the bogie frame. Twin Flexicoil springs on each side of the bogie form the secondary suspension and permit the bogie to twist, rotate and move sideways relative to the body of the locomotive. Braking is by compressed-air cylinders pressing the blocks directly on to the wheel rims. Sand boxes to aid adhesion on damp rails are provided for each direction of running.

1 *Axles and wheels*
2 *Axle-suspended asynchronous traction motor*
3 *Motor axle support and gear case*
4 *Primary suspension and horizontal link to bogie*
5 *Brake blocks and cylinders*
6 *Secondary suspension*
7 *Sand boxes*
8 *Bogie frame*

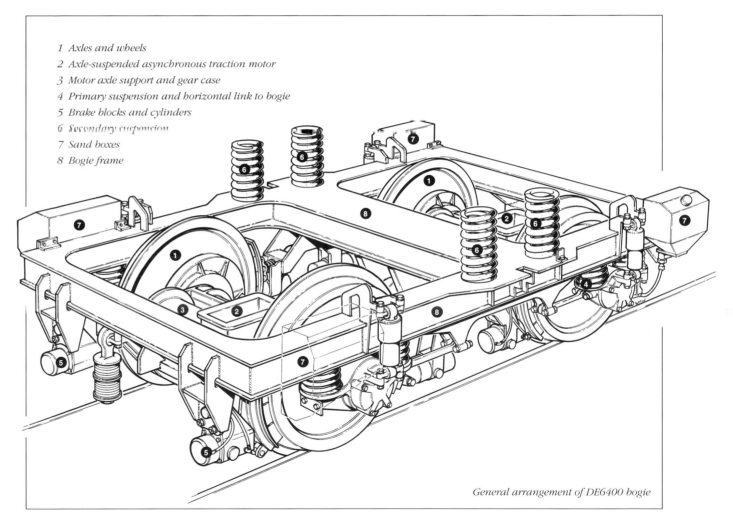

General arrangement of DE6400 bogie

Coupling on buffer-beam of DE6400 locomotive

Power unit

The main power unit is a supercharged Motoren-und-Turbinen-Union Frederichshafen (MTU) four-stroke engine, rated at 940 kW or 1040kW at 1800rpm. It was twelve cylinders in a 90° Vee, each with a capacity of 3.96 litres. The pistons, which are water-cooled, are 165mm in diameter with a stroke of 185mm and a compression-ratio of 12.3:1. A turbocharger followed by an intercooler supplies the combustion air to the unit. A roof-mounted fan draws cooling air for the radiator through the side filter-panels towards the front of the locomotive. The diesel engine drives a six-pole ABB three-phase alternator, rigidly bolted to it. Although operating at a lower loading, its rating is 1200kW (1610hp) at 1400V.

A three-cylinder HARZ diesel producing 14kW (19hp) at 1500rpm provides the auxiliary power. Some of the other auxiliary systems on the locomotive, such as the air compressors, have hydrostatic drives, the speed of which does not depend on the voltage output of the main electrical system.

After rectification from three-phase to direct current at 1400V, the output from the diesel alternator is fed to the air-cooled inverters in the equipment case in front of the cab. Here it is converted to the three-phase supply needed for traction purposes, the frequency being variable between 0 and 170Hz. Each of the four axles is powered by an ABB traction motor and, as the locomotives are designed for relatively low-speed running, the motors are of the nose-suspended variety. This increases the unsprung weight on the axles, but the penalty is small because a three-phase asynchronous motor is much lighter than the dc alternative of the same power. Air ducted through the bogie frames to blowers in the body cools the motors. A microprocessor controls the operation of the power-electronics in the inverter to provide the correct voltage and frequency to match the requirements set by the driver's controllers.

As with the shuttle locomotives, asynchronous traction motors were chosen because they do not require commutators. There should thus be no trouble with internal condensation in cold weather if a locomotive has been standing in the open and then has to enter the warm, humid atmosphere of the Tunnel. The motor characteristics also provide a high tractive effort when starting; this was demonstrated during system trials when an NS locomotive was able to move a 2400-tonne train from rest up a 1 in 90 gradient.

1 Main controller
2 Brake equipment
3 Speedometer
4 TVM 430
5 Gauges
6 Reverse selection
7 Emergency push button
8 Auxiliary switches
9 Touch-screen radio coding
10 Radio telephone

Driver's controls of the Eurotunnel DE6400 locomotive

Scrubber Units

Special precautions are required before any internal-combustion engine can be operated safely in a confined space. Plenty of oxygen is required, and the toxic content and any unpleasant smell must be removed from the exhaust gases. This is difficult to achieve in long tunnels, but much experience was gained during construction of the Channel Tunnel when constant monitoring of the air purity in the tunnels proved that the temporary ventilation system would allow a limited number of small diesel construction locomotives to be operated underground.

A catalytic converter and scrubber units have been provided to purify the exhaust emissions of the higher-powered DE6400 locomotives. The converter, which is similar to those now fitted to conventional cars, is mounted on the locomotive as part of the silencer system. The scrubber units are carried on a special four-wheeled flat wagon positioned immediately behind the locomotive, and between them when two are in use; this deals with the exhaust from both locomotives simultaneously.

The precious-metal catalyst in the converter transforms any poisonous carbon monoxide in the exhaust into carbon dioxide, which is a normal component of the atmosphere. From the converter, the exhaust gases travel through a stainless-steel pipe to the scrubber unit; bellows provide the necessary flexibility over the couplings to allow for track curvature.

The scrubber units, which were developed by Percevaut at its works near Paris, were used during the construction of the Villejust Tunnel on the TGV-Atlantique line. More recently they were employed with the former BR Class 20 locomotives that worked construction trains in the Channel Tunnel.

As the photograph below shows, the scrubber unit consists of three parts. In the exchanger, the incoming gases at 450°C are cooled by those leaving the unit, to avoid overheating the scrubber and the absorber. The scrubber contains 3.5 tonnes of a solution of sodium carbonate, better known as washing soda because it was

DE6400 diesel-electric locomotive coupled to scrubber unit

used for cleaning before the invention of detergents. An electric pump at the end of the unit circulates the solution through a series of sprays. These wash out any oxides of nitrogen left in the exhaust gases, and also remove any fine carbon particles; these form the soot that appears at times in the exhaust of a diesel engine, particularly when the power output changes.

Diesel fumes also smell somewhat so, after leaving the scrubber, the gases pass through baskets of active carbon in the absorber. These remove the residual smell, as well as any remaining traces of sulphur- and nitrogen-containing compounds.

Before being discharged into the Tunnel through the top of the unit, the gases pass through the other side of the heat exchanger, which warms them again. This prevents condensation as they emerge into the cooler air of the Tunnel where the presence of clouds of 'steam' would be undesirable.

Auxiliary generators on each scrubber unit power the pumps and cooling fans. Like the locomotives themselves, the scrubber wagons conform to the UIC 505.1 loading gauge, so enabling them to operate over much of the continental railway network if required.

Maintenance Trains

To enable Eurotunnel to operate the various types of train safely through the Tunnel, more than 300,000 items of fixed equipment have had to be installed, not counting the track and the overhead electrification system. All these items, as well as the Tunnel itself, have to be inspected at intervals, and many of them have to be serviced, maintained or renewed. A large proportion of the vital fixed equipment is in the rail tunnels, and access to these requires the engineers to take 'possession' of an 18km length of one tunnel between crossovers, while trains continue to operate through the other on the single-line system. In the early hours of weekday mornings it is possible to do this without causing inconvenience to those wanting to use the Tunnel. On some occasions, when possession of half of one of the crossovers is required, the single-line operation will extend for two-thirds the length of the Tunnel (36km).

In size, the fixed equipment items range from a simple lighting fitting to lengths of rail or a transformer, and the equipment required to service, maintain or replace them is correspondingly varied. Each item has its own schedule for inspection and servicing, which is available from a special bilingual computer system,

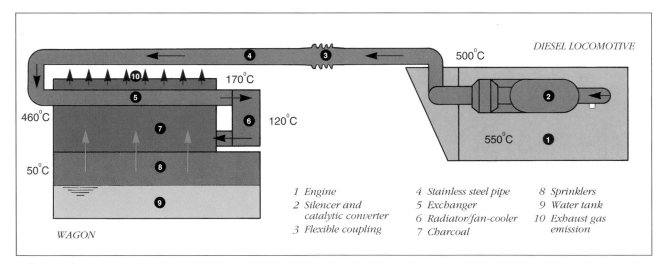

1 Engine
2 Silencer and catalytic converter
3 Flexible coupling
4 Stainless steel pipe
5 Exchanger
6 Radiator/fan-cooler
7 Charcoal
8 Sprinklers
9 Water tank
10 Exhaust gas emission

Schematic diagram of scrubber unit

which monitors the work carried out. The Tunnel will very quickly become the most heavily-used railway in the world, and this means that some heavy items of equipment will have to be replaced within a comparatively short time. The point-blades, for example, are likely to require changing every year, and it is predicted that significant rail replacement will be needed after seven years' operation. As it is not possible to undertake all the latter at one time, this work is expected to begin after three to four years in the first instance, which will even out the process, making it more cost-effective.

Each maintenance train has to carry all the equipment, staff and stores needed for the work during that particular possession. Most national railway systems, with hundreds of miles of line to maintain, have fleets of specialised railway wagons for the use of their maintenance engineers. These are backed up with road vehicles which are often used to deliver small items, as well as staff, to the operational site. In the Tunnel such a system would be impossible or uneconomic, and a very unusual method of operation has been adopted, based on the equipment used for intermodal trains.

Eurotunnel has purchased 15 flat-wagons, similar in principle to the SNCF's 'Multifret' ones used for containers and swap-bodies. They were constructed near Como in Italy by Costamasnaga SpA, and each is capable of carrying up to three specialist 'modules', as shown on page 96. These correspond to containers, and can be lifted on and off the flat-wagons by fork-lift trucks in the maintenance areas at each terminal. Thirty-two modules, of seventeen different types, were constructed by SOCOFER at its factory in Tours. They are 6m or 9m long, except for two 12m tanks.

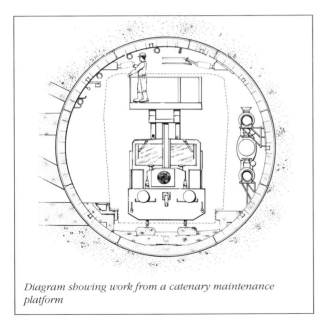

Diagram showing work from a catenary maintenance platform

While some modules were designed for very specific purposes, others are capable of being used by all trades working in the Tunnel. The most important of these are the amenity modules, which have a small workshop, complete with air-compressor, as well as messing and transport facilities for the staff. The flat wagons are fitted with swing-up, automatic couplers of the modified BSI RK900 type, and have air-brake pipes on each side, although only one set is used at a time. (This simplifies the task of coupling them up in the Tunnel.) Maintenance trains are normally hauled through the Tunnel by one of the DE6400 diesel-electric locomotives, which is attached to its Percevaut scrubber unit; the train can operate at speeds of up to 100km/h using the normal TVM 430 signalling system.

In the course of a normal possession, work sites could be as far as 18km apart, which makes it difficult to optimise the use of staff and equipment during this short period. Many inspection jobs also require the equipment to move along the Tunnel during a possession, and this would be very difficult with a single locomotive for each train. Accordingly another very unusual arrangement has been adopted, which uses a number of other smaller locomotives. These are hauled into the Tunnel as part of the train, and, as each working site is reached, one of

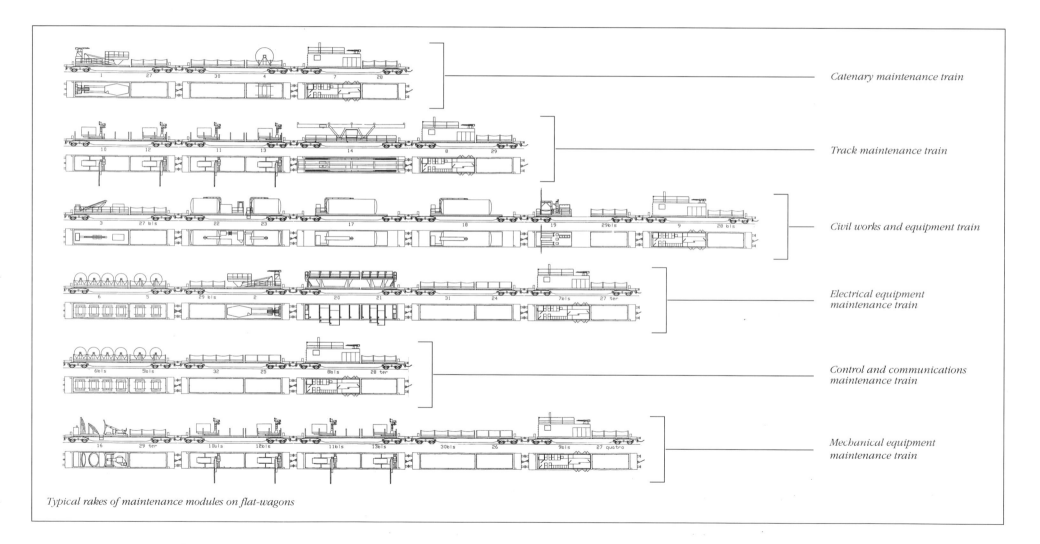

Catenary maintenance train

Track maintenance train

Civil works and equipment train

Electrical equipment
maintenance train

Control and communications
maintenance train

Mechanical equipment
maintenance train

Typical rakes of maintenance modules on flat-wagons

them, complete with its own wagons and modules, is uncoupled and left behind. During the possession each of these sub-trains can move about to suit the work to be done. Under these conditions they are permitted to move at speeds of up to 30km/h, under the *Marche à vue* (Move on Sight) rules, as they do not have TVM 430 cab-signalling equipment.

An even more unusual arrangement has been adopted to enable one or more of these locomotives to be controlled remotely from various positions along their train. The control panel can be plugged in at either end of each flat-wagon, as well as on the roof of the amenity module and in the hydraulic-lift tower used for inspection and maintenance work in the top of the Tunnel. Speed is limited to 15km/h when operated in this way, but the system provides all the controls to move the train safely and position it exactly where needed for each task.

The operating cycle for the maintenance train is for it to be made up during the day in the form required for the following night's operations. This takes place in one of the special sidings in the two terminal areas. Each of these is provided with standing space for the modules not required, as well as easy access to the stores building. After the departure of the last operational train

to use the affected section of the Tunnel, the maintenance train moves in. After all the necessary safety precautions have been taken, such as de-energising and earthing the overhead wires, and closing the piston-relief dampers, Railway Control hands over the possession of that section to the person in charge of the maintenance train. At the end of the work-session, normally four hours long, the train is reformed, and permission is obtained for it to leave the section. Once more running under TVM 430 control, it travels to the terminal on the opposite side of the Channel, runs round the turning loop, and stables in the maintenance siding at that end. On the following night it will be scheduled to work in the other tunnel as it makes its way back. Staff who finish up in the 'wrong' country return home in one of the shuttles.

The two additional small locomotives have been constructed by Schöma (Christoph Schöttler Maschinenfabrik GmbH) taking parts from a pair of construction-gauge ones used by TML. Little more than the power-trains have been retained. These consist of a F.W. Deutz 10-cylinder F10L 413FW diesel engine, with a rating of 170kW (230hp) at 2300rpm. This drives a 5000 Series Clark transmission via one of the same manufacturer's oil converters. Originally this gave four

speeds in each direction by engaging or releasing different clutches, but the top gear has now been isolated. When being towed by the DE6400 locomotive, all the clutches are disengaged and the locomotive is able to be towed at 100km/h. Given the low power rating, and the excellent ventilation conditions in the tunnels, these locomotives do not require any exhaust-treatment equipment.

The service tunnel has a number of functions. It is used for access to the technical equipment located in the cross-passages and in the equipment rooms along it. It also provides fresh-air ventilation for the rail tunnels, and acts as a 51km-long safe haven if a shuttle or train has to be evacuated. The Service Tunnel Transport System, or STTS, enables staff to reach every point in the Tunnel, if necessary at short notice.

When the Tunnel system was being designed, it was initially intended to use a narrow-gauge railway system for access. However, although this would have provided guidance as well as speed, the system lacked the flexibility of a road and rubber-tyred vehicles. Accuracy of lateral positioning in a small tunnel is essential, and, after extensive testing, it was decided to use specialised rubber-tyred vehicles whose steering, and therefore their position in the Tunnel, can be controlled by a buried-wire guidance system. The initial fleet of purpose-built, double-ended STTS vehicles was subsequently supplemented with lighter vehicles, known as LADOGs, derived from commercial runabouts used extensively throughout continental Europe.

STTS Vehicles

Twenty-four STTS vehicles have been constructed. Each consists of a framework that connects a cab and power unit at each end, enabling it to carry a variety of different 'pods', colour-coded to indicate their purpose. Their primary role is maintenance, but they are also used for fire-fighting and other emergency purposes. Special pods for each different type of service are inserted from the side, after blocking up the vehicle to prevent its suspension sinking as the weight is transferred. The payload is 2.5 to 3 tonnes.

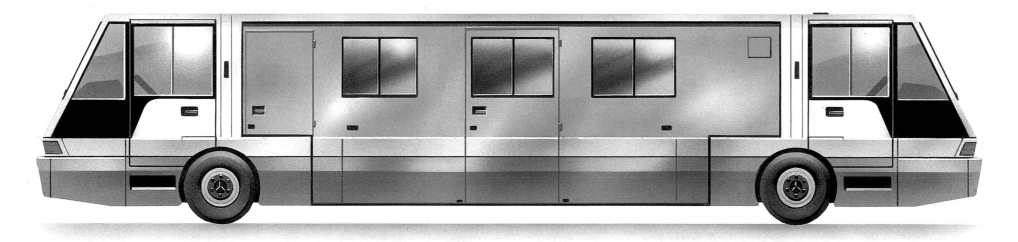

Service Tunnel Transport System (STTS) vehicle with a maintenance pod

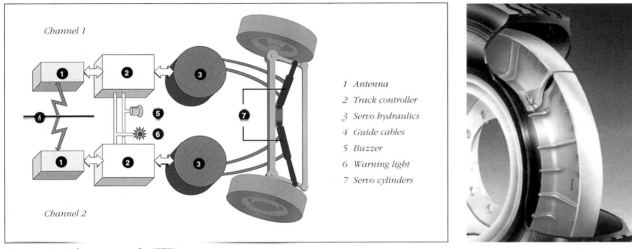

Channel 1

Channel 2

1 Antenna
2 Track controller
3 Servo hydraulics
4 Guide cables
5 Buzzer
6 Warning light
7 Servo cylinders

Automatic guidance system for STTSs

Internal arrangement of 'run-flat' disc

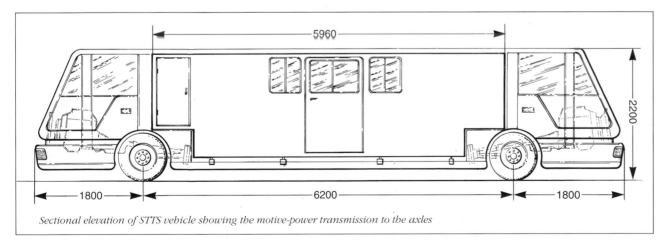

Sectional elevation of STTS vehicle showing the motive-power transmission to the axles

The STTSs are driven from the leading end. They are too long to be turned in the Tunnel, so when they need to reverse the driver changes ends after centralising and locking the steering and shutting the motor down. The power unit at the 'new' leading end is activated, and the vehicle can then be driven back to its starting-point.

Two pairs of continuous wires run under the floor of the service tunnel. Sensors on the vehicles enable them to lock on to the left-hand wire of the pair so that the driver does not have to steer. In this mode they can travel at up to 80km/h. If they are being steered manually, speed must be kept below 50km/h.

Each vehicle has two Daimler-Benz OM 602 diesel motors (as used on the Mercedes 190), individually rated at 62kW (83hp) at 3400rpm. Each motor drives the nearer axle through a Daimler-Benz W4A 028 automatic transmission; only one is used at any time. The original intention was to provide an electric drive as well, but the ventilation in the service tunnel has proved to be so good that there is no need for this added complication.

Each rubber-tyred wheel is fitted with an internal 'run-flat' disc, enabling it to continue if it suffers a puncture. The design is derived from the pneumatic-tyred railcars and coaches that operated fairly extensively between the two world wars on the French railways. An

Inserting a pod on an STTS

STTS with fire-fighting pod

example is on display in the railway museum at Mulhouse in eastern France.

Two STTSs vehicles are on duty in the Tunnel for fire-fighting purposes at all times. Staff also deal with routine duties during their shifts. A back-up vehicle is also constantly available.

Light Service Tunnel Vehicles (LADOGs)

The need for these vehicles became apparent while the Tunnel was being built. A larger fleet of vehicles enables more efficient use to be made of the staff who maintain the interior of the Tunnel and the wide variety of equipment it contains. Without the light vehicles, the STTS vehicles would have to operate a 'bus service' at

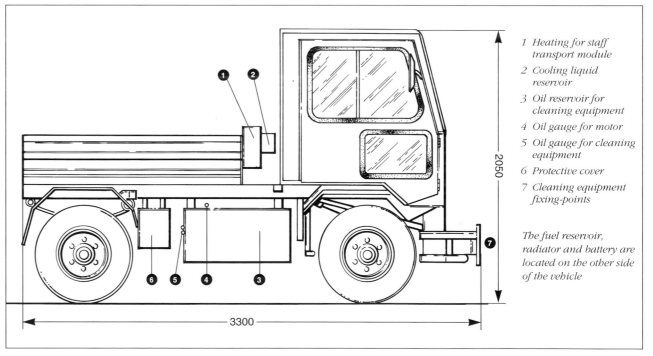

1 Heating for staff transport module
2 Cooling liquid reservoir
3 Oil reservoir for cleaning equipment
4 Oil gauge for motor
5 Oil gauge for cleaning equipment
6 Protective cover
7 Cleaning equipment fixing-points

The fuel reservoir, radiator and battery are located on the other side of the vehicle

Light Service Tunnel Vehicle (LADOG)

Method of offloading a pod from a LADOG (above and below)

set intervals, delivering a succession of people and equipment to different points in the Tunnel. Having completed a particular job, the person concerned would have to wait for the next return working.

A fleet of fifteen LADOGs was purchased to get round this restraint and to assist maintenance and other work in the terminal areas. Built by Nordrach at its factory in the Black Forest, they are used extensively throughout Europe. The LADOGs have a short wheel base, with hydrostatic drives to each wheel; all four wheels can be steered, the minimum turning circle being only 3.4m. This enables them to make a two-point turn in the width of the service tunnel, the first move being in reverse. However, most drivers generally carry out three-point turns, as they do in the open. For normal driving, the rear-wheel steering is locked; power is split between the four wheels to avoid one end getting bogged down on soft ground in the open. Experience has shown that a differential lock is not necessary, even when the vehicle is operating in deep snow.

Each LADOG is powered by a 40kW (54hp) Volkswagen diesel motor, with separate injection-chambers for each cylinder. This gives a cleaner fuel burn at a lower temperature, helped by the reduced compression ratio. The power output for the given swept volume is also kept low, and the motor works at relatively modest rotational speeds. Maximum speed in the Tunnel is 50km/h. Unlike the STTS vehicles, the steering of the LADOGs cannot be locked to the buried guide-wire.

Their hydrostatic power arrangement enables LADOGs to be fitted with auxiliary equipment powered by the same means. Some are provided with rotating sweeping brushes, washers, or vacuum drain-cleaners, and all have attachments for snowploughs. While the shuttles themselves are not affected by severe weather, it is necessary to keep the roads and platforms in the terminal areas clear of snow. A light fork-lift attachment is also available at the front of the vehicle.

LADOGs are not provided with 'run-flat' wheels, unlike the large STTS vehicles. However, each carries a foam-injection cylinder to reinflate a punctured tyre, enabling them to leave the Tunnel. Spare tyres are available, for them and for the large STTS vehicles, at the base just outside each portal.

The LADOG fleet consists of two different types of vehicle; the eighteen intended primarily for use inside the service tunnel are slightly shorter. Their model number is AS129, and their lifting cabs for access to the motors can be raised inside the Tunnel. A variety of

A LADOG, left, and an STTS alongside each other in the service tunnel. The pairs of buried guide cables can be seen in the tunnel floor

pods of up to 1 tonne in weight can be accommodated on the rear of the vehicle, including a personnel-carrier. These are jacked off and supported on legs when not in use. The weight of an empty LADOG is 2.5 tonnes, half the weight of a loaded STTS vehicle. The LADOGs used in the Tunnel are 3.3m long, l.25m wide and 2.05m high.

Since road vehicles are driven on opposite sides of the road in France and the UK, a standard rule of the road had to be adopted for the road vehicles in the service tunnel. It was agreed that they should drive on the left, and the drivers therefore sit on the right. Because of the slight danger that a continental driver might subconsciously steer to the right when another LADOG was approaching, the Safety Authority required warning sensors to be fitted to each vehicle. These alert the driver if a vehicle strays significantly to the right across the Tunnel.

Eurotunnel's passenger-vehicle and freight shuttle services occupy half the capacity of the Channel Tunnel. The other half is used by a variety of international through-trains: Eurostar day passenger services, European night services and freight trains. The daytime passenger services are operated by European Passenger Services (EPS, a British Rail subsidiary), SNCF (*Société Nationale des Chemins de Fer Français*) and SNCB/NMBS (*Société Nationale des Chemins de Fer Belges/Nationale Maat-schappij der Belgische Spoorwegen*). DBAG (*Deutsche Bahn AG* – the newly-combined railways from east and west Germany) and NS (*Nederlandse Spoorwegen*) are joint operators of the night services with SNCF and EPS.

One of the 300km/h Eurostar trains that link London with Paris and Brussels passing through the Folkestone Terminal

Eurostar services

Some thirty Eurostar services a day in each direction are planned to run through the Channel Tunnel, linking Paris and Brussels with British Rail's purpose-built Waterloo International station in London. From Waterloo, trains will use the existing tracks at speeds of up to 160km/h as far as Eurotunnel's Folkestone Terminal. Having travelled through the Tunnel, they will join the new TGV Nord Europe route at Frethun, just

Waterloo International station

outside the Calais Terminal, where a newly-built station serves the Calais area. Opened in 1993, the new line runs for almost 320km via Lille to the outskirts of Paris at Gonesse, a short distance from the Gare du Nord terminus. Brussels services use the TGV line as far as a point south-east of Lille, where they transfer to the existing Lille-Brussels route until the high-speed line between the French/Belgian frontier and Lembeek, just south of Brussels, has been completed.

The fastest Eurostar trains take three hours for the London-Paris journey, and fifteen minutes longer to reach Brussels. They will travel at up to 300km/h on the French high-speed line. From 1995 a limited number of through services will link Paris and Brussels with Edinburgh via the East Coast Route, and with Birmingham and Manchester. The Belgian high-speed line is due to come into service during 1996; this will reduce the London-Brussels journey time to two hours forty minutes.

A British high-speed link between the Folkestone Terminal and London has been under discussion for many years, and both the financing and the various alternative routes proposed have provoked much controversy. The government has chosen a route from Folkestone to a second international terminal at St Pancras, cutting 33 minutes from Eurostar's timings. Its development, by Union Railways, depends on attracting private capital.

Customs and immigration controls will generally be undertaken on the train, but special facilities have been built at Waterloo International. On regional services all controls will be on the train.

Ownership of the 31 Eurostar trains operating between London and Paris/Brussels is split among BR, SNCF and SNCB/NMBS in the ratio 11:16:4. The trains have a '2 + 18' formation, and consist of two identical halves, each of which is numbered separately in the Class 373 series. BR has ordered an additional seven trains, each with four fewer coaches, for its services north of London.

Supply systems

Eurostar trains are required to operate on three separate supply systems. The SNCF lines between Paris and the Channel Tunnel and the Tunnel lines themselves are electrified at 25kV ac, as will be those of the Belgian high-speed line. Although there are a number of differences in the design of the 25kV overhead wiring, the same pantographs can be used throughout. The existing Belgian lines are electrified on the overhead

system, but at 3000V dc. This requires a separate pantograph on the Eurostar locomotives, as well as additional equipment to feed power to the traction motors, and to meet the train's lighting, heating and other internal demands. Because of the limitations of the lower voltage and the capacities of the lineside supply system, the maximum power output in Belgium is currently less than half that on 25kV; this is not unduly significant because of the lower speed limits on Belgium's conventional lines.

The third supply system is located in England, on the lines between the Folkestone Terminal and Waterloo International. Here Eurostar trains will operate on the third-rail system, which is energised at a nominal 750V dc. Retractable shoe-gear on the power bogies picks up current from the third rail; the need to provide these, together with the equipment required to enable the locomotives to use this low-voltage supply, has complicated the trains' design. Voltage drops are much more common on the third-rail supply, and there are gaps in the conductor rails at junctions. These, coupled with the supply arrangements on the British Rail network feeding the sub-stations between Folkestone and London, restrict the power output of the Eurostar trains to less than a third of their potential in the Tunnel and in

Dollands Moor, a holding siding for through rail freight situated adjacent to the Folkestone Terminal. The Eurostar train leaving the siding would normally use the through line to the Tunnel on the right

exchange yard, running first over the British third-rail system as far as Dollands Moor near Folkestone and then through the Tunnel under the 25kV ac catenary. The other Class 92s will haul the overnight passenger services from London or Glasgow through the Tunnel to Calais. (The Plymouth/Swansea services will be diesel-hauled west of London, Kensington Olympia, since those routes are not electrified.) Two locomotives, one at each end of the train and each with its own driver, will be used through the Tunnel. This will enable the train to be reversed or divided for evacuation purposes in the event of an emergency.

The Class 92s have a Co-Co wheel arrangement, their bogies being based on those used for the Class 60 diesel-electrics built by Brush for BR. However, the wheelbase has been lengthened to provide space for the third-rail pick-up shoes; each bogie has a pair of shoes and a single one on each side, so making a total of twelve. Generally only six will be in use, because the third rail is normally laid on one side of the track only. When the locomotive is operating from the overhead system, the shoes are retracted; they are raised by springs, but are held down in the working position by compressed-air cylinders.

Operating currents are much higher with the 750V system, and this, together with the use of direct current, causes arcing when a train passes over the gaps in the third rail at sub-stations and points. Microprocessor control of the power circuits of the Class 92s detects these gaps and notches the power back to reduce the arc as the second bogie comes off the third rail. As on Eurotunnel's shuttle locomotives, three-phase ABB motors with identical converters are used; however, because the Class 92s are limited to a maximum speed of 140km/h, the motors are of the 'nose-suspended' type, so avoiding the complications of a flexible drive-train.

The locomotives have a maximum output of 5MW (6700hp) on the 25kV system, but this is reduced to 4MW (5360hp) when they are working on the third-rail system with its supply limitations. A maximum tractive effort of 400kN (90,000lbf) is available, but this is only used as a 'boost', the normal output being restricted to 360kN (81,000lbf) because of the UIC coupling limitation. This would enable a single locomotive to haul a 1600-tonne train from Willesden to Calais via Redhill and Tonbridge, as well as over the southbound climb to Beattock Summit from Glasgow, although freight trains in excess of 1300 tonnes gross will be double-headed by two Class 92s through the Tunnel itself. A number of emergency performance requirements were also specified. These included taking a 1600-tonne train northbound up Beattock Bank on the 1 in 75 gradients from a dead stand, as well as hauling a train plus a dead locomotive from Kilometre 23 in the Tunnel to the Folkestone portal on the 1 in 90 gradient at a restricted speed of 30km/h.

The Class 92s are capable of being operated in multiple, either as a pair coupled together or marshalled at each end of a train if the coaches are fitted with the necessary cabling. In the former case their combined tractive effort is automatically restricted to 360kN to avoid damage to the train's drawgear.

As with the other types of motive power operating through the Tunnel, the design of the Class 92s conforms to the safety requirements of the Intergovernmental Commission as developed for the Eurotunnel shuttle locomotives; however, for reasons of economy there are two traction units per locomotive. The interior of the locomotive is arranged in three zones, the two traction ones being over the bogies, and all are provided with appropriate fire-extinguishing equipment. As the traction zones represent the primary risk areas, they are enclosed between bulkheads capable of withstanding a fire for thirty minutes.

Part Two

Tunnel Infrastructure

concrete, forming a continuous 'arch' 170m long, 19m wide and 12m high (after lining), and the cavern was excavated inside them. The spoil inside the 'arch' and the rail tunnel linings previously installed were then demolished and removed.

Cross-passages, piston relief ducts, plant rooms

Cross-passages every 375m and piston relief ducts every 250m were generally constructed by traditional hand tunnelling methods. The cross-passages, which provide links for services between the service tunnel and the rail tunnels, were also provided with doors to control access and ventilation.

Each piston relief duct has a butterfly-valve damper at one end. Looking like overgrown satellite TV dishes, the dampers are closed when maintenance is taking place, so preventing trains passing in the other tunnel forcing or sucking air through the ducts.

In addition, other excavations between the tunnels were needed for various types of operational technical equipment such as control rooms, sub-stations and pumping stations. These were subsequently fitted out with specialist equipment brought down the tunnels.

Getting ready to place a damper in one of the piston relief ducts between the rail tunnels

Once the tunnels had been completed, the construction railway was replaced by the standard-gauge permanent way, and catenary was installed to provide power for the locomotives, the power cables being fed from the supply systems at the French and British terminals. The signalling system (see chapter 11) is not based on conventional trackside colour-light installations. Instead the required information is transmitted directly into the locomotive cabs via a system that automatically limits the speed if the driver fails to respond. All that can be seen in the Tunnel are the 'flag' section-markers that indicate the start of each separate block section and trackside equipment that transmits information electronically to the trains.

Such equipment is generally sufficient to operate a railway, but in the longest undersea railway tunnel in the

Stretch of rail tunnel showing walkways, cabling, pipework, permanent lighting and piston relief duct

world a variety of special services and equipment is needed. Normally the tunnels are not lit; however, the maintenance and emergency lighting system comprises approximately 20,000 fittings on the sides of the tracks nearest the service tunnel. The two walkways are for use by maintenance personnel, but not of course while trains are running through that particular section of tunnel, and also serve to contain a train in the event of a derailment. The inner walkway also enables passengers to transfer to a train in the other tunnel via cross-passages and the service tunnel in the very unlikely event of their own being immobilised. There are also special radio antennae to provide communications between the control centres and train crew.

In the rail tunnels a drainage pipe under the track leads to the pumping station. Although water seepage is very low, it is also necessary to allow pumping capacity for tunnel-washing, fire-main operation and accidental water-pipe leaks. Twin cooling pipes circulate chilled water from equipment at both coasts to absorb some of the heat generated by the passage of trains (see page 120).

In the undersea sections of the service tunnel, the main discharge pipes from the pumping stations are slung from supports in the Tunnel roof. Any water from the roadway drains to the pumping-station sumps via the under-roadway drainage pipe. In addition to the lighting, power supply and communication cables, and a loud-speaker system, two wires buried below the concrete running surface of the service tunnel provide guidance for the specialist road vehicles used in it (see chapter 6).

Ventilation

During ordinary operations, the ventilation system provides the fresh-air supply for the tunnels; the flows are shown in green on the diagram below. Two fan stations, one situated at the top of the Shakespeare Cliff ventilation shaft, the other next to the Sangatte shaft,

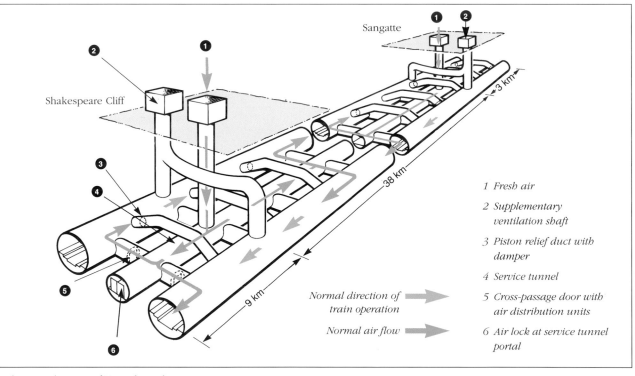

1 Fresh air

2 Supplementary ventilation shaft

3 Piston relief duct with damper

4 Service tunnel

5 Cross-passage door with air distribution units

6 Air lock at service tunnel portal

Normal direction of train operation ➡

Normal air flow ➡

Schematic diagram of Tunnel ventilation system

Aerial view of the Sangatte site (see also page 113). The shaft, with stairs, is in the foreground. Behind it are the water reservoir (for fire-fighting), the diesel-electric emergency generator, the cooling pumps and the cooling plant. The ventilation plant is centre right, and the supplementary ventilation plant centre left

pump air into the service tunnel; the flows are 88 m³/sec at Shakespeare Cliff, 73m³/sec at Sangatte. An air-lock in the service tunnel at each portal, consisting of two doors 55m apart, prevents air escaping from the ends and maintains it above atmospheric pressure. Air escapes into the two rail tunnels through distribution units in the doors of every third cross-passage, so achieving equal distribution along the tunnels. This system ensures that the fresh-air supply in the service tunnel remains at a higher pressure and separate from that of the rail tunnels. In the event of smoke in a rail tunnel, the service tunnel would provide a continuous 'safe haven'.

As the shuttles travel through the Tunnel at speeds of up to 140km/h, they push air ahead of them, and also create a partial vacuum behind the rear locomotive. To reduce the drag this causes, the piston relief ducts, which connect the two rail tunnels at 250m intervals over the top of the service tunnel, allow the displaced air to pass from the front to the back of the train via the opposite tunnel. The potential peak air velocity through these ducts is so great that restrictors have been fitted to ensure that the blast emerging into the other rail tunnel does not unduly affect a passing train. Although the piston relief ducts 'short-circuit' much of the air movement, a general flow is still induced along each tunnel in the direction of

travel, so supplementing the normal ventilation system.

The supplementary ventilation system, which is only brought into operation during maintenance periods or in an emergency, augments the air supply, using two additional fans at the ventilation plants. The British fans have a capacity of 260m³/sec, while the French ones can deliver 300m³/sec. Ducts connect the fans through a system of valves to either or both rail tunnels, and the fans themselves are reversible so that each of them can blow air into or extract it from the tunnels. If dust, fumes or a fire should occur, the fans and valves will be set up to deliver the maximum amount of fresh air to where it is needed, and to remove smoke from where passengers may be located.

The entire ventilation system, including the direction of the flows from the supplementary fans, and the position of the valves in the piston relief ducts and cross-passage doors, is operated from both the Folkestone and the Calais Control Centres. This enables the atmosphere in the affected rail tunnel to be cleared as rapidly as possible.

Cooling

A great deal of electrical energy is used in the Tunnel for traction and other purposes, nearly all of which is ultimately degraded to heat. While some heat will pass through the Tunnel walls or will be carried out in the flow of ventilation air, a cooling system is needed to remove the rest. Without it the temperature in the Tunnel would slowly rise to an uncomfortable level.

In each rail tunnel two cooling pipes, each 400mm in diameter, are fixed on the 'outer' side. (The UK underland pipes have a diameter of 300mm.) Cold water from chilling plants situated close to the coastal shafts circulates through the pipes, flowing seaward along one pipe as far as the half-way point, then back towards land along the other. As it circulates, the water will gain heat; on its return to the chilling plant it passes through one of

four large heat-exchangers, which cools it and returns it to the Tunnel. On their low-temperature side the heat-exchangers are cooled by a circulating refrigeration system; this includes a battery of fan-coolers that finally eject the heat from the Tunnel into the atmosphere. The pipes are equipped with cut-off valves that close automatically in the event of a burst, and can also be shut by remote control from the Control Centre.

The British chilling plant, which has a thermal capacity in excess of 28MW, is situated at the base of Shakespeare Cliff, on the previous colliery embankment and on land reclaimed from the sea by dumping spoil

from the Tunnel. This large building, with its banks of fan-coolers, can be seen from trains between Folkestone and Dover. The French installation, close to the former construction shaft at Sangatte, is smaller because the French cooling circuits are shorter on the land side. Between them the two plants will maintain the temperature in the Tunnel within the range 25-35°C.

Drainage

For most of their length the tunnels were bored through solid beds of chalk marl. This is remarkably impervious to the flow of water, and the amount seeping into the tunnels between the lining segments proved to be even less than expected. At places, however, notably the first few seaward kilometres from Sangatte, fractures and fissures increase the inflow of water, which, due to reverse osmosis, has only about half the salinity of sea water. There is also a very limited inflow from the water table in the underland sections of the tunnels.

All water entering the Tunnel, together with any spillages, must be collected and pumped out. The core of the drainage system is the sumps and pumping station at each of the three low points of the tunnel. (The Tunnel itself is not flat since its route follows the layer of chalk marl.) One low point is in mid-Channel, 22km

The cooling plant at Sangatte

from Sangatte and 16 from Shakespeare Cliff; the others are located landward of the two undersea crossover chambers, 9km from Sangatte and 6 from Shakespeare Cliff respectively. These collect water from the drain laid beneath the track in each rail tunnel, and the corresponding one in the service tunnel.

The drainage system has substantial buffer capacity to cope with potential problems such as a burst in one of the cooling pipes. In this event, despite the cut-off valves, a considerable quantity of water would escape and have to be removed. There is also capacity to isolate spillages of liquids that should not be discharged in the normal way, by means of a 'dangerous goods sump'. Although inflammable liquids are banned from the Tunnel, in very unusual circumstances one of the diesel locomotives or other maintenance motors could, for example, lose fuel.

Each pumping station consists of an extensive three-dimensional network of tunnels (as shown in the diagram of the mid-Channel installation right) constructed in two symmetrical halves. Duplication of equipment ensures that maintenance work, or an emergency, does not put the whole installation out of action. The first pair of pumping-station tunnels is located between the rail tunnels and the service tunnel;

each is about 100m long. One end contains the electrical sub-station that provides the power to operate the pumps and other equipment, and also houses the anti-

surge tanks; their function is to prevent damaging 'water-hammer' in the long pipes leading to the surface. The motors that drive the main pumps are also located in the

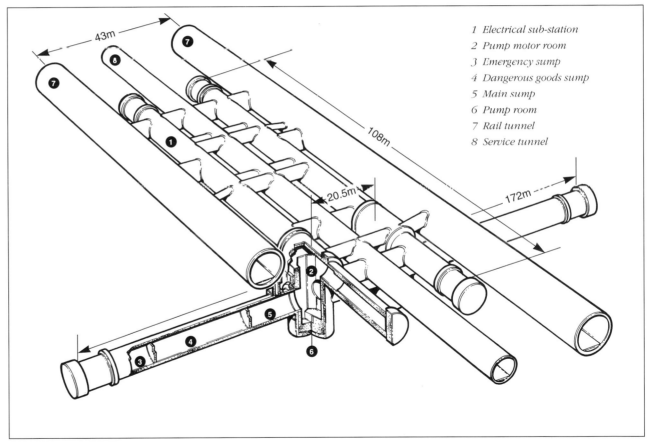

1 *Electrical sub-station*
2 *Pump motor room*
3 *Emergency sump*
4 *Dangerous goods sump*
5 *Main sump*
6 *Pump room*
7 *Rail tunnel*
8 *Service tunnel*

Schematic diagram of mid-Channel pumping station

same tunnels, at the top of the vertical shaft from the pump room which lies approximately 18m below; this positioning ensures that the motors remain well above the water level in the sumps. As an additional precaution, some of the pumps could continue to operate even if their motors were completely submerged.

The sumps themselves are located towards the bottom of the vertical shafts, stretching sideways for some 86m on both sides of the centre-line of the service tunnel. The section between the two vertical shafts is the dry sump. Internal walls divide each outer section into three chambers. Nearest the pump room is the main sump; the water flowing along the rail and service tunnel drains reaches this by gravity. Beyond the main sump are the dangerous goods sump and the emergency sump. Drainage from the tunnels can be diverted into whichever of these is appropriate.

Each pump room contains two pumps, driven by vertical shafts from the motors above them, capable of emptying the sumps in half an hour against the very considerable delivery head (see table below). The lowest pumping-station sump is 120m below sea level, giving a delivery pressure from the pumps of more than 12 bar. From the pumps, the delivery is into three rising mains located in the crown of the service tunnel; space is available to install a fourth main if this should prove necessary. The rising mains discharge at Sangatte and Shakespeare Cliff where the drainage water is treated to ensure adequate quality, the clean water being discharged into the local drainage system or the sea.

The entire drainage system is operated remotely from the Control Centre. Sensors constantly transmit information about the levels in the sumps, and monitor the position of the valves and the action and flows of the pumps.

Fire main

The Channel Tunnel is unusual in having a high-pressure fire main throughout its length, to enable crews to fight any fire that might occur. It is located in the service tunnel, and hydrants are provided in both rail tunnels at intervals of 125m. These outlets have connections which can be used by both French and British fire-fighting crews. In an emergency they would bring the necessary hoses, and specialised discharge equipment for the foam system, by dedicated STTS vehicle (see chapter 6).

A fire hydrant in a rail tunnel

Location	Sump capacities (m³)			Pumping capacity (m³/h)
	Main	Emergency	Dangerous Goods	
British side	2 x 150	2 x 600	2 x 140	4 x 895
Mid-Channel	2 x 120	2 x 1100	2 x 550	4 x 735
French side	2 x 90	2 x 830	2 x 270	4 x 560

Pumping-station capacities

The Folkestone portal from the track alongside the Terminal used by passenger and freight through-trains

A single standard-gauge track runs through each of the two rail tunnels under the Channel. This gauge of 4 feet 8½ inches (1.435m) dates back to the early days of the railways, and was adopted elsewhere when British engineers laid the first lines in many other countries. The common gauge means that, provided they can cross the Channel, there is nothing to prevent continental trains running on British track, and vice versa. However, the larger continental loading gauge – that is, the width and height to which rolling stock is built – means that most continental trains are too wide or too high to clear British platforms and bridges.

When British Rail metricated its civil engineering, the width of the gauge was reduced by 3mm, from 1.435 to 1.432m, to improve the riding at high speeds. Some continental lines also have slightly narrower track gauges, but such small differences do not prevent through running between the continent and Britain.

The flat-bottom rails used in the Tunnel are of the UIC60 type (which means that they conform to the standards laid down by the Union Internationale des Chemins de fer and weigh 60kg/m). Such heavy rails are used extensively on the European mainland, including the French high-speed lines.

On the British side, five 36m lengths of rail were welded together electrically by the flash-butt method at the British Steel Corporation's rolling-mill at Workington, Cumbria. The resulting 180m 'strings' were delivered to the Folkestone Terminal site, laid in the tunnels and finally welded *in situ* using the 'Thermit' process (known in France as the *aluminothermique* method). Much the same process was followed for the track delivered to the French side; most of the welding took place at the SNCF workshops at Moulin Neuf-Chambly, north-west of Paris, with part being done by SNCB/NMBS staff from Schaerbeek, north-east of Brussels. Welded rail can buckle in hot weather, and in the open precautions have to be taken to prevent this. However, in the relatively constant temperature of the Tunnel, this is not a problem.

Early in the next century the Tunnel is expected to become one of the most intensely used stretches of railway in the world. The frequency of trains and shuttles will allow little opportunity to undertake major track relaying, although some key track components could be changed as frequently as once each year. The design specification thus required the track supports to have a life of fifty years, although it was accepted that the springs that hold the rails to the sleeper blocks might have to be changed after twenty-five. The Sonneville system was selected; this uses pairs of reinforced-concrete blocks to support the rails at 600mm intervals. R. Sonneville and Henry Girod-Eymery, co-founders of the French STEDEF track-laying company, invented this system, which was developed further in the USA. Some 334,000 Sonneville blocks were manufactured in the concrete plant at the Sangatte construction site, where tunnel linings had previously been made.

To provide resilience, the rails sit on 'H'-shaped pads of microcellular ethyl-vinyl-acetate (EVA) with a grooved surface; complex screw fastenings, as shown opposite, attach the pads to the blocks. Nylon clips and EVA pads provide electrical insulation to ensure the proper operation of the track-circuits in the damp and salty conditions of the Tunnel. A rubber 'boot' surrounding

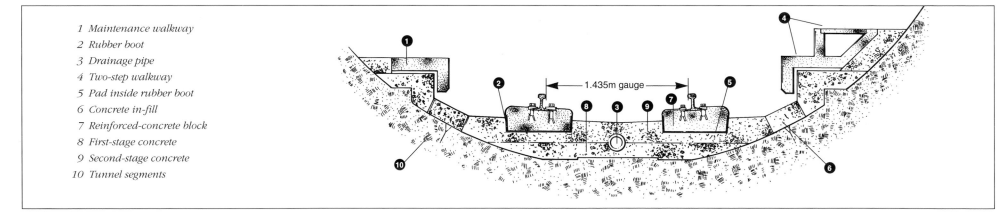

1 Maintenance walkway
2 Rubber boot
3 Drainage pipe
4 Two-step walkway
5 Pad inside rubber boot
6 Concrete in-fill
7 Reinforced-concrete block
8 First-stage concrete
9 Second-stage concrete
10 Tunnel segments

1.435m gauge

Cross-section of base of rail tunnel, showing details of construction

the bottom of each sleeper block provides additional insulation.

After the tracks of the narrow-gauge construction railway had been removed and the tunnel interior had been cleaned, 'first-stage' concrete was laid on the bottom of each tunnel. To begin with, the track assemblies were placed on this. Then the track was positioned accurately, and 'second-stage' concrete was laid round and under the blocks, making the entire

trackbed a solid structure. Experience on the Paris Metro and other systems has proved that this method does not require a metal 'spacer' to connect the blocks, as happens with ballasted track. This system permits a more accurate alignment, reduces noise and does not run the risk of corrosion or breakage.

At the British end, the trackside walkways, already formed in the Tunnel linings, were completed after the 'first-stage' concrete was laid. This did not happen on

the French side, because when the lining segments were put in place the final 'key' segment was at a different place in each ring. Hence it was not possible to incorporate supports for the walkways in the lower segments, in contrast with the British system. Before the 'first-stage' concrete was laid, the French segments were drilled to take the reinforcing rods for the walkways and the walkways themselves were cast. This provides a continuous 'trench' in which the trains travel. If there is a

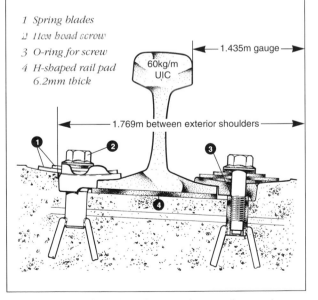

1 Spring blades
2 Hex head screw
3 O-ring for screw
4 H-shaped rail pad 6.2mm thick

60kg/m UIC

← 1.435m gauge →

← 1.769m between exterior shoulders →

Fastening system for rails in the Tunnel. On modern track the tops of the rails lean towards each other

Rail fastening

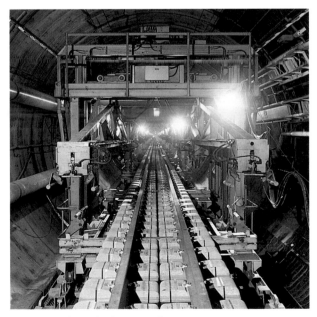

Rail strings being laid in Tunnel using gantry supporter

derailment, the walkways keep the trains upright and prevent them coming into contact with cables or other equipment in the Tunnel.

Low aerodynamic resistance is another very important benefit of the Sonneville system. In the confines of the Tunnel, some of the air displaced by the front of the train rushes back under and alongside the wagons to help to fill the vacuum created at the rear.

The more freely this can take place, the less energy is required to propel the train forward. While this itself provides an energy saving, in the Tunnel all such turbulence is also converted into heat, which the cooling system has to remove; this in turn requires the expenditure of yet more energy in the refrigeration plants.

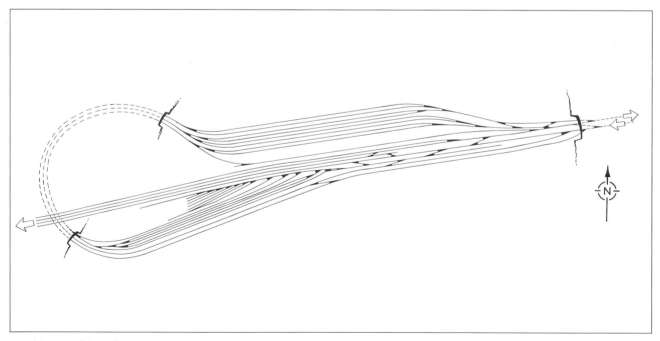

Track layout of the Folkestone Terminal

A former British Rail Class 20 diesel-electric locomotive operating the first train to use the crossing in the UK undersea crossover

In the undersea crossover chambers, the pointwork is laid on long wooden sleepers instead of separate concrete blocks. The track and pointwork are surrounded with rubber seals as a protection against derailments and to help to seal the central sliding doors. Wooden sleepers are also used in the loop tunnel at the Folkestone Terminal. Elsewhere in the terminals, conventional tie-bars connect pairs of 'Duobloc' concrete sleeper blocks. This type of track is used extensively in France and other European countries, although not in Britain, Italy or Germany.

The track-laying train at work in the UK undersea crossover

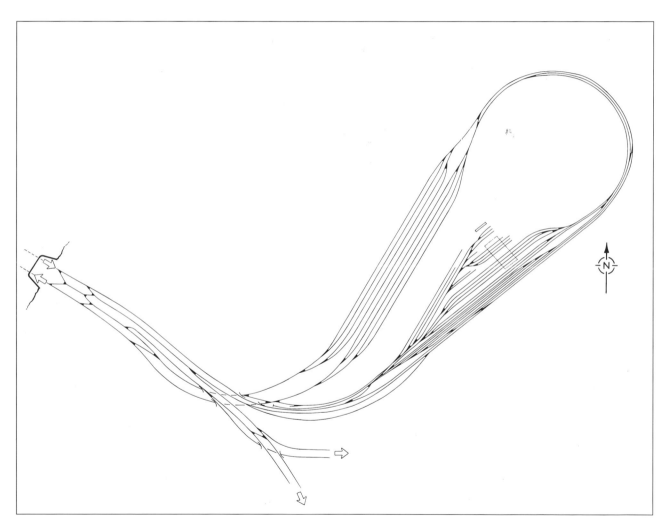

Track layout of the Calais Terminal

Chapter 11

A section-marker at the end of a platform in the Folkestone Terminal

The Treaty of Canterbury (see Introduction) requires Eurotunnel to install signalling equipment that will provide twenty paths per hour in each direction through the Tunnel. This means that two trains of the same type (eg passenger-vehicle shuttles, Eurostar services) must be able to run at full speed only three minutes behind one another. Even though the maximum speed in the Tunnel is only 160km/h (for Eurostar services), not much more than half that attained on the TGV lines, the small headway between the trains necessitates a very sophisticated signalling system. This has been adapted from the system developed for the 300km/h TGV Nord Europe route, from Paris to Lille and Calais, and is known as TVM 430 (TVM = *Transmission Voie Machine*, or track-to-train transmission).

Track circuits

Every signalling installation has to be provided with information on the precise location of each train. In most present-day systems this is achieved by passing low-voltage electric currents through the wheels and the rails, forming what is known as a track circuit. Current is fed into the rails at one end of each block section, and there is some sort of electric indicator at the other. If there is nothing on the line, the current flows through the indicator, but if there is a train in that particular section the current is short-circuited through the wheels, and nothing reaches the far end. In its simplest form the indicator then displays a sign 'Train on Line' in the signal box. It will be noted that such a system is designed so that if anything should go wrong with it – the source of power fail, for example – it will indicate that there is a train present, even if there is not. It is one of the fundamentals of all signalling systems that they are designed always to 'Fail Safe' in this way.

In place of a simple indicator, the detector at the far end of the track circuit can be made to provide an input to a complex signalling system. Many power signalling systems are operated by rooms full of relays, which change the signal aspects automatically to 'Danger' behind any train. They similarly provide sufficient 'Caution' warnings at other signals beforehand to ensure that every train is kept clear of the one ahead. Throughout the world there are many miles of plain track that are operated completely automatically in this way, with the signalman normally leaving it to itself. Where there are junctions, track circuits are also used to ensure that points are not moved while trains are passing over them, while other relays ensure that signals cannot be cleared to permit two trains to approach on conflicting routes.

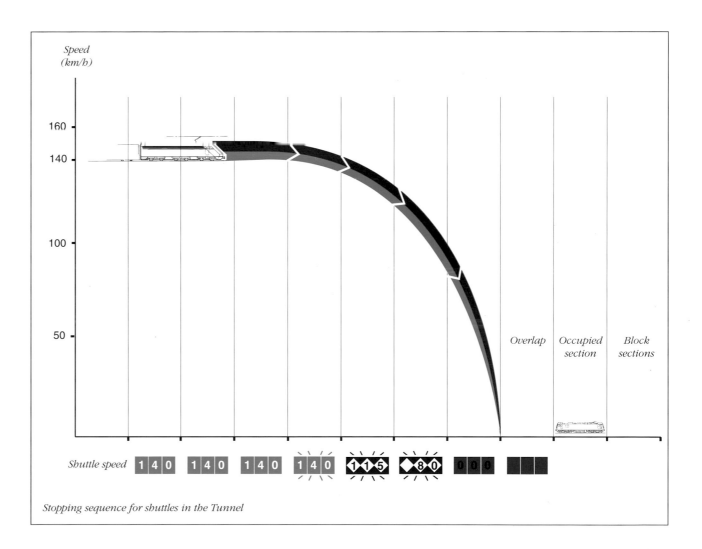

Stopping sequence for shuttles in the Tunnel

Nowadays it is possible to monitor and operate all the relay rooms along a line from a central control, using computers. As well as showing where each train is on a graphic diagram, they can also automatically direct each of them along its correct route. All of them are constantly prevented from running into the one ahead, and are similarly protected from those following along behind. The computer systems not only check themselves continuously, but others are on 'hot' standby to take over if anything should happen to the one in charge.

TVM 430

TVM 430 is a cab-signalling system, the locomotive driver receiving the necessary information from indicators in the cab rather than from fixed signals on the lineside. In the tunnels, TVM 430 operates with 500m-long track-circuit blocks. A blue and yellow section-marker, fixed to the tunnel wall, indicates the start of each section, rather than the colour-light signal used on conventional track. The marker, which is the only external signal in the tunnels, tells the driver that the train is moving from one block section to the next; this is where the signal aspect shown in the cab may change or a speed reduction may become mandatory. A

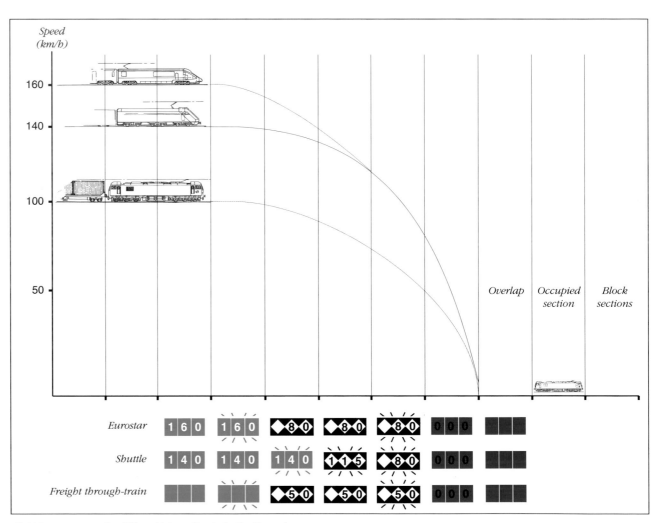

Stopping sequences for different types of train in the Tunnel

series of illuminated numbers on the driver's desk conveys the vital information on how fast it is safe to travel, and the automatic train control (see chapter 13) ensures that the actual speed does not exceed this by more than a few km/h. If the train's actual speed is higher at any time, the brakes are applied automatically. When there is a stationary train ahead, the permitted speeds are graded so that a driver following the proper braking procedure slows down smoothly, and comes to a gentle halt, a complete section clear of the obstruction.

A shuttle travelling at 140 km/h needs 1500m – three block sections – to make an ordinary service stop. The diagram on page 129 gives a visual representation of the way a shuttle would approach another stationary train in the tunnel. The driver of a shuttle running under clear signals has the figures 140 illuminated on his desk in white on green squares; so long as the 140 is visible, the shuttle can continue at full speed. One section before braking has to begin, the display starts to flash so as to alert the driver to the coming change. As the next section-marker is passed, the display alters to 115 in black figures on white lozenges; this is the target speed to be achieved at the end of that section. (Whenever the permitted speed changes like this, up as well as down, the driver also receives an audible warning.) Because in

this particular case a further change is coming, the display flashes. As the next block section is reached, the figures change to a flashing 80, and then, at the one after that, 000 is shown in black on a red background; this tells the driver that the train must stop just before the next section-marker. At any point in this sequence,

The transmission loops for one of the fixed TVM 430 beacons on the track

should the driver fail to slow the train down according to the pre-set instructions, the brakes are automatically applied. Were the train to over-run the final stopping-point, the display would change to three plain red squares, and an emergency brake application would be made. Should a shuttle have to assist a train ahead out of the Tunnel, the Control Centre will give special permission for it to pass this point at a low speed.

By 1995 three different types of through-train will use the Channel Tunnel, besides Eurotunnel's passenger and freight shuttles. There will be the Eurostar services from London and beyond to Paris and Brussels, the overnight passenger trains, and the freight through-trains (see chapter 7). All these trains have different maximum speeds in the Tunnel, and each has its own version of the cab-signalling display. Eurostar services and other passenger trains will be able to run at a maximum of 160 km/h in the Tunnel, and so need an extra block section in which to stop. The drivers will receive a flashing green 160, followed by three sections of 80, with only the last one flashing.

There is no overall fixed maximum speed for freight trains, as this will depend on the type of wagons included. The freight 'All Clear' cab signal display will thus consist of plain green squares. The braking systems on the freight trains are not as sophisticated as on the other types, so longer stopping distances are needed from a given speed. The sequences of indications for all three types of train coming to a stop are shown on page 130.

A train using a crossover must slow down from its normal speed to travel across the points. As the train approaches, the driver receives an appropriate sequence of warning signals, so ensuring that the train reduces speed. The final display is a white-on-black 60km/h speed indication, telling the driver the speed over the junction. The same system applies in the terminals as trains accelerate away from the platforms or brake on approach.

Originally track circuits were operated by a simple battery housed in a pit between the rails. Today high-frequency, coded signals are used, which also provide information to the train. Sensor coils in front of the train's leading wheels pick up these messages, which are decoded by the train's computers. Additional information is supplied at fixed locations along the track by transmitting loops, known as beacons, laid between the rails; other sensors on the leading locomotive pick up the signals from these.

The TVM 430 system has been developed from those used on the earlier French TGV routes. When the first section of the line from Paris to Lyon was opened in 1981, the signalling system provided eleven continuous sets of information; this was increased to fourteen on the TVM 300 system for the TGV Atlantique in 1989. Thanks to contemporary electronics, TVM 430 is immensely more powerful. It can provide no less than 2^{21} sets of information. The capacity of this system enables many other commands to be given to the locomotives, such as the need to slow down for a temporary speed restriction.

To enable the computer to apply the brakes if the train is going faster than the signalling allows, an accurate indication of speed is required at all times. This is obtained in digital form from the series of impulses generated in a magnetic coil as a toothed wheel passes it. These detectors are mounted on the locomotive's axles.

The vital NS1 relay racks in the Folkestone Terminal signalling poste

The British electrical sub-station in the Folkestone Terminal

The electrical system is required to provide the Channel Tunnel systems with power for traction purposes as well as for additional demands such as pumping, lighting and ventilation. Because the national grids of Britain and France are not synchronised, no direct ac connection is possible between them. There is a link across the Channel, but this is a dc one, originally installed to share power at times of peak loading but now more generally used to import cheaper power from France.

The Channel Tunnel's electrical system has therefore been designed to take single-phase power from both the French and British national three-phase grids in a manner that does not adversely affect the operation of either grid or of the dc link. The system's traction needs are high, since the power requirements of the shuttles (both passenger and freight) are much greater than those of conventional trains. In addition, the intensity of operation in the Tunnel, with trains running at up to every three minutes in each direction, demands a reliability and complexity of power supply not generally provided on other railway systems.

Many railways throughout Europe have adopted a 25kV ac supply, using a catenary. This can supply the power necessary for the heavy demands of the present rail network and all foreseeable future lines. This system is used on the French TGV lines and on all new electrification programmes on Britain's main-line railways, and was therefore the only possible choice for the Channel Tunnel.

On the former Southern Region lines in south-east England, however, power is supplied through a third rail at 750 volts dc. Special arrangements have been made to enable passenger through-trains to change between the two systems without stopping. In the long term, the plan is that the majority of passenger through-trains, and some freight through-trains, will use the new high-speed line between London and the Tunnel. This would be provided with a 25kV power supply, thus achieving a continuous 25kV supply between north of London and

Paris and Brussels as well to many other destinations already electrified at this voltage.

In the 750-volt third-rail area of south-east England, there are normally feeder sub-stations every 5 to 8km, depending on the density of traffic. On the Folkestone to London line used by Eurostar services, the existing spacing has been halved to meet their high power requirements. The 25kV system permits a much greater distance between feeder stations. The usual distance on British and French main lines is 40 to 65km; the Channel Tunnel falls within this range. However, as it is set to become the most heavily loaded railway in the world, and also includes long adverse gradients, special arrangements are necessary to transmit the traction

power supplies from both ends and to ensure that the working voltage remains between 19.5 and 27.5kV.

Catenary

Locomotives collect current from the contact wire using a pantograph. This has metallised carbon strips on its top surfaces; on the Channel Tunnel locomotives, springs keep the pantograph in contact with the lower surface of the hard-copper contact wire with a static force of 70 Newtons (N) (16lbf); this can increase to a maximum dynamic figure of 210N (47lbf).

'Droppers' from the upper catenary cable support the contact wire and ensure that it remains at a roughly

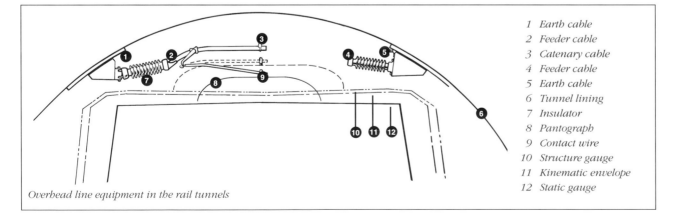

1	Earth cable
2	Feeder cable
3	Catenary cable
4	Feeder cable
5	Earth cable
6	Tunnel lining
7	Insulator
8	Pantograph
9	Contact wire
10	Structure gauge
11	Kinematic envelope
12	Static gauge

Overhead line equipment in the rail tunnels

Insulated support for feeder cable and earth cable in Tunnel

constant height above the rails. In the tunnels the catenary is formed from a stranded copper cable; elsewhere in the UK a reinforced aluminium type is used. Specially designed insulated registration-arms for the contact wire permit adjustment about various axes; these are used to maintain the alignment of the contact wire, which, as is normally the case, zig-zags slightly relative to the track to even out the wear on the pantograph's contact-strips. In the tunnels the attachments for the catenary and the registration arms are combined; one of each is mounted on an insulator fixed to the roof every 27m.

Like the contact wire, the catenary is tensioned with a force of 20 kilo Newtons (kN) (4500lbf); this is normally achieved by means of weights on pulleys at the ends of each length. However, in a tunnel the geometry is much more difficult than in the open, where the weights are hung vertically from lineside masts. The system adopted is similar to that installed by Spie Batignolles on the Cairo Underground.

The tension in the contact wire is the same as that used on the 300km/h TGV lines; this is appreciably more than the latest 11kN standard adopted by BR (although not much higher, proportionally, when the larger cross-section area of the wire is taken into account). Like that of the TGV lines, the Tunnel's contact wire has a cross-section of 150sq mm; this is almost 50 per cent greater than the BR standard, but additional transmission capacity has been provided over and above this. The cross-section of the supporting catenary is larger still, at 185sq mm.

In the tunnels the catenary cable and contact wire are normally installed in sections of 1.2km, with successive lengths of the contact wire overlapping to enable the pantograph to slide from one to the other and maintain constant contact. Track-sectioning equipment is installed at some overlaps in order to enable lengths of catenary to be electrically isolated for maintenance. On an ordinary railway the necessary high-voltage switch-gear is normally installed in cabins alongside the track or on masts; in the Tunnel the special rotary switches are located near the top of the arch.

With mainland high-voltage ac electrification it is necessary to install a neutral section between each pair

Tension system in the tunnel for overhead wiring

Catenary arrangement and protection on the Calais Terminal

Neutral section

of feeder stations; without this the railway's catenary could form part of the national electricity distribution system, or interconnect two phases. In the case of the Tunnel, the French and British national electricity ac supply systems must never be directly connected, as already mentioned. Neutral sections consist of a short earthed section of contact wire, separated from the live stretches on each side by an insulated glass-fibre rod, on which are threaded ceramic beads. Its mechanical characteristics are such that a pantograph is not unduly disturbed, even when running at full speed.

In UK practice, and generally in France as well, power normally travels from the feeder station to the neutral section along the contact wire and catenary. However, the huge traction demands in the Tunnel uniquely necessitate the provision of two entirely separate 25kV copper feeders, each with a cross-section of 240sq mm, in each of the two rail tunnels in order to maintain the operating voltage within the required limits. The feeders are cross-connected with the catenary and contact wire, and so differ from the latest arrangements on the TGV lines, where the feeder sometimes operates with the opposite polarity. (The latter arrangement must be connected to the catenary via autotransformers; known as the 2 x 25kV system, it is used when it is not

possible to locate the feeder stations close enough together.) On most British lines, booster transformers are installed at intervals, to transfer the current returning through the rails into the return conductor, which, like the transformers, is mounted on the lineside masts. This system was not adopted in the Tunnel. Instead, the rails are earthed at intervals into the chalk marl that surrounds the Tunnel, although two earth cables are also mounted in the top of each tunnel. (At the conclusion of the undersea tunnelling, when the heads of the British TBMs were buried below the line of the Tunnel, the resulting large mass of metal was used to provide a good earth.) Using either boosters or the 2 x 25kV system would have increased both equipment and heat generation in the Tunnel, and hence the capacity needed for the cooling system. The additional feeders used in the Tunnel have the added advantage of enabling all the power to come from one side of the Channel in an emergency.

Power Supply

It is customary to generate power in three-phase form, with, effectively, three separate alternators interlaced inside the one machine. This evens out the torque required to keep the rotor turning, and the output is

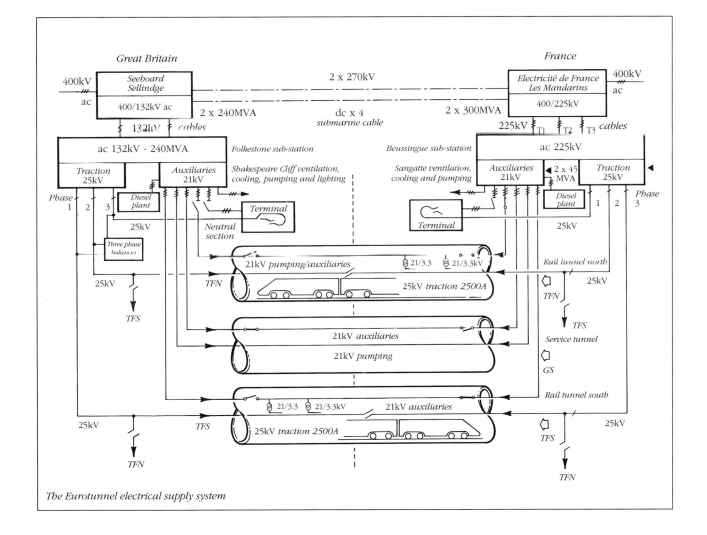

The Eurotunnel electrical supply system

then transmitted using sets of three conductors, as is apparent when one looks at the pylons of any national grid system. Any consumer that takes an appreciable amount of power will use all the phases, since most motors with an output of more than a few horsepower are three-phase. Only domestic consumers normally take their power from a single phase, adjacent houses being supplied from a different phase to even out the loading.

Electric railways clearly fall in the category of major users, but it is difficult to provide a three-phase supply to a moving train. In 1901 the world's first 160km/h speed was achieved by a German electric locomotive that used a cumbersome pick-up system from a series of three contact wires alongside the rails; however, this arrangement could not have been used on a commercial railway. Until 1980 the Italian railways used a simpler three-phase system at speeds of up to 130km/h; there were twin overhead wires, and the track formed the third phase. However, such systems are now confined to a few short mountain railways. There is thus the problem of ensuring that the single-phase power demands of a railway do not upset the loadings on the rest of the grid.

In most places where 25kV electrification is used, the feeder stations, taking power from the high-voltage grid lines, can be located in major industrial areas; a different phase is used on each side of a feeder station. The degree of imbalance between the phases is thus insignificant compared with the total local demand. The Channel Tunnel requires on each side between 100 and 200 megawatts of power, which necessitates further precautions being taken in both countries, particularly because there is no major industrial power usage in the vicinity of the Folkestone terminal.

On a conventional railway it is not feasible to use a different phase for the up and down tracks; crossovers and junctions make it impracticable to maintain absolute separation between the tracks, and such an arrangement would thus create short-circuits. However, the two rail tunnels under the Channel are separated throughout, except for the two undersea crossovers where the overhead wires on the crossing tracks are earthed when the dividing doors are closed. Neutral sections have also been provided over the 'scissors' crossing. It has thus been possible to use a different phase in each tunnel at the two ends, so helping to balance them. The catenary in the Folkestone Terminal area is energised from the remaining phase of the national grid, so neutral sections are necessary in the two rail tunnels on the seaward side of the crossover situated just inside the portal, and also

on the seaward side of the crossover outside the French portal. Neutral sections are also installed in the middle of the tunnels, and these normally separate the British and French systems. Since remote-controlled switches are installed to bridge the neutral sections in certain emergencies or during maintenance, a computerised system interlocks all 25kV switches; only five configurations are possible, of which only one can be used at any time.

While three-quarters of the power demand in the Channel Tunnel is for traction purposes, supplying other

requirements from the third phase coming into the sub-stations at each terminal evens out the loading still further. However, other power (for pumping, ventilation, lighting etc) is sent down the cables in the service tunnel on three phases at a voltage of 21kV, and is transformed for ac use to voltages of 3.3kV, 400V and 230V, and rectified to 110V and 48V dc at various points underground.

Despite these arrangements, problems with voltage variations and the production of 'harmonics' could still arise in east Kent. This would be particularly likely if one

British Rail Class 87 locomotive, City of Chester, carries out the first live tests on the 25kV supply system, Folkestone Terminal, Spring 1992

of the landward sections of the Tunnel were closed for maintenance and several trains were following each other up the gradient towards Folkestone. Accordingly a complicated Steinmetz 'balancer' (or thyristor-controlled filters) has been installed at the sub-station in the Folkestone Terminal. This will ensure that any imbalance between the phases is contained within the Eurotunnel

system and will not affect any of Seeboard's other users. Three systems for 35MVAR and a stand-by one are installed in the UK sub-station.

By contrast, the French grid system in the Calais area is close to several high-power generating stations, which makes it less sensitive to imbalance between the phases. The connection with the French 400kV grid

system at Les Mandarins, 2.5km from the Calais Terminal, is via two autotransformers. (The French terminal of the 2000MW submarine-cable dc energy-exchange system between France and the UK is also at Les Mandarins.) At the Eurotunnel sub-station, two single phases are used for the two traction supplies to the tunnels, and the third for the terminal catenaries; the auxiliaries are fed from all three phases. There is also the facility to switch any part of the load to either of the feeder circuits, including, as explained above, the entire Tunnel system's catenaries and cables, and, if necessary, the Folkestone Terminal.

The power supplies in France reach the Beussingue sub-station, close to the French portal, by cables at 225kV. On the British side of the Channel, Seeboard similarly provides power through underground cables from Sellindge, at the other end of the submarine cables, but at only 132kV. These supplies are both duplicated, and are routed sufficiently far apart to prevent both sets being accidentally cut by, for example, someone using a digging machine. In each case Eurotunnel has had to provide the equipment at the point where its supplies leave the grid systems, together with the cable connections between these sites and the Eurotunnel sub-stations in the terminals; these total 14km in Kent and

Les Mandarins sub-station, where the Eurotunnel electrical system connects with the French national grid, and also the terminal of the France-UK energy-exchange system

Aerial view of the French portal and the Beussingue cutting, with the French electrical sub-station alongside

2.5km near Calais. The capacity required is enormous. Initially a total of 160 megawatts will be needed on each side of the Channel, equivalent to the peak demand of a city with 250,000 inhabitants.

Although the British and French ac national grid systems have to be kept separate because the phases are not 'synchronised', there are facilities, as explained above, to enable the whole of the Tunnel's electric supply to be provided from one side of the Channel, should the other country's grid shut down. The 275kV dc cable link between Les Mandarins and Sellindge, known as IFA 2000, can itself provide sufficient power from one national grid in case of loss of power on the other, thus feeding one sub-station from the other national system. In the extremely rare event of both 'going out' simultaneously, 21kV three-phase auxiliary diesel generators at Sangatte and Shakespeare Cliff would be started, initially to feed the lighting system, then the ventilation and pumping circuits. Any additional power available would be used for the control and communication supplies, which in any event have their own three-hour battery back-up on automatic standby. Their limited output means that these auxiliary generators cannot supply traction current.

The heart of the Channel Tunnel is a complex and busy railway. For long periods it will operate at full capacity, with shuttles, Eurostar expresses and freight trains running in each direction at intervals of as little as three minutes. At each terminal a complex and extensive network of tracks includes junctions with the national railways. The three 50km tunnels themselves contain the large quantity of equipment required to ensure uninterrupted running through the two rail tunnels and along the service tunnel roadway. All this has to be operated and maintained under traffic, 24 hours a day throughout the year. Train running must be to the highest standards, and any incidents must be dealt with rapidly and effectively.

To ensure the necessary levels of safety, security and service, three main types of control are provided. The first covers the railway system, the second deals with the road traffic within each terminal, while the third provides a focal contact point for outside organisations in the event of any major incident.

Railway control

Prime responsibility for the entire railway system in the tunnels and terminals is taken by the conspicuous control centre on the Folkestone Terminal, which looks rather like the bridge of a ship, complete with mast. The similarly equipped control centre on the Calais Terminal is on permanent standby, ready to take over from

Folkestone if necessary. In addition to the control of the trains by means of the signalling system (see chapter 11), this responsibility includes the tunnels' ventilation, drainage and power supply, as well as all other operations and maintenance that take place in the tunnels.

'Control' means having the information available to enable safe and efficient decisions to be made. Much of the operation is automatic, in that equipment is switched on or off in response to particular information fed back from measuring equipment. However, all such operations, and the procedures they follow, are designed to be 'fail safe'. This means that, if there is any equipment failure, the system immediately assumes its

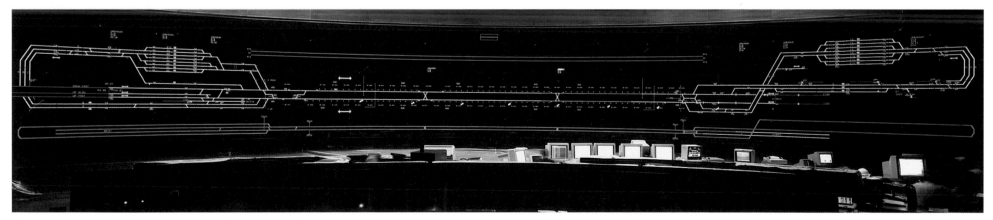

The mimic diagram of the Channel Tunnel rail system in the Folkestone railway control room

most restrictive mode. For example, if the signalling pulses through the rails were to stop, the computer on the locomotive would immediately stop the train, without any action by the driver. That is probably the most dramatic example of a 'fail safe' system, and in many other cases it is not vital for everything immediately to be brought to a halt. Information would be provided about the cause of failure, which would then be analysed and appropriate action taken by those in control. The staff on duty at each Control Centre are in constant communication with each other and with other staff throughout the system.

The Folkestone railway control room is at the rear of the building, partially below ground. Here the controllers sit at three curved rows of desks, with the mimic diagram of the entire system displayed on a curved wall in front of them. Should a fault put this room out of action for any reason, responsibility is immediately transferred to the Calais railway control room, where the same information and work stations are available, but without the mimic diagram.

Each Control Centre handles its own terminal shunting activities, away from the main shuttle and rail lines. Any movements involving the main operational rail lines are co-ordinated with the Folkestone Control Centre.

The Folkestone Control Centre, heart of the Channel Tunnel system. The blurs along the sea signify Channel maritime traffic, visible because of the long exposure of this photograph

Road traffic control

Trains using the Tunnel are all operated by the trained railway personnel of Eurotunnel or the rail companies. By contrast, road vehicles are the responsibility of many thousands of individual drivers, whose movements are spread over large areas of the two terminals. Road traffic is thus under local control, and the road traffic controllers in each Control Centre have a direct view on to a large part of the terminal, including the allocation lanes where vehicles wait to board the shuttles. Video cameras provide additional information and monitor out-of-sight locations where congestion or problems might arise. At both terminals the road traffic controllers work from the top level of the glazed Control Centre towers.

Control systems

Broadly speaking, all the control systems operate on the 'by exception' principle; staff are alerted only when something unexpected happens. Computer-driven systems assist the work of the controllers. On the railway side, the signalling system automatically keeps trains apart in the tunnels; the main control system also operates the running lines on the terminals so that train movements conform to the operational timetable.

While Le Shuttle operates on a 'turn-up-and go' system, and booking and reservation are not required, the shuttles themselves run according to a prearranged timetable, which also allocates paths to the passenger and freight through-trains. As on every railway system, more paths are available than are required for the service. This allows the rail traffic controllers to alter schedules and add extra trains as demand or other traffic conditions dictate. The path allocated to a particular shuttle or through-train is calculated to provide the most efficient combination of power consumption and speed profile for each particular type of train or shuttle. The on-board signalling equipment logic determines the limits within which the train is actually driven.

Traffic planners prepare the details of the timetable daily, taking into account constraints of rolling stock and staff availability, as well as the Tunnel's capacity and maintenance requirements, and feed these into the system. The computers already know the expected

The Calais Control Centre

arrival time of an international through-train. If it is running to time, its path through the terminal and into the Tunnel is cleared automatically. If it is running late, the controller must consider whether to amend the sequence of trains entering the Tunnel in accordance with previously established procedures.

Once a shuttle or through-train has entered the Tunnel, the signalling system takes over control. The track circuits (see chapter 11) constantly indicate its location and identify it on the mimic board in the Control Centre. When one section of a tunnel is closed

for maintenance, the movement of trains through the remaining rail tunnel, on single-line working, is also controlled automatically from timetable information in the computer.

Because there is no prior booking, sufficient shuttles must be provided to meet the demand within as short a period as possible. While pre-planning is possible in the light of experience, the Control Centre monitors the system and changes the number of shuttles in service to match demand. If an extra shuttle is required at short notice to deal with an unexpected

surge in traffic, rather than signal it through the system from the control panel, the timetable is altered. This establishes the best path for the new shuttle and enables its actual running to be adjusted should any delays occur.

The Control Centre also monitors and operates many hundreds of items of fixed equipment installed in the tunnels. For example, if one rail tunnel is closed to traffic for maintenance the configuration of the system must be changed in a number of important ways. First, the dividing doors in one or both of the undersea

The road traffic controllers' view over the allocation lanes on the Folkestone Terminal

crossover chambers have to be opened to enable the crossover tracks to be used. The catenary may have to be isolated and earthed if work is to take place nearby. Finally, the dampers in all the piston relief ducts along the section of tunnel concerned must be closed to prevent sudden air movements that could affect people working in the Tunnel.

Monitoring is a constant process, and only when something is not performing correctly are the railway controllers warned. If more than one item requires attention, the computer system presents an order of priorities. The system also provides video displays of the equipment concerned and lists of other items to check. A log is automatically kept for later investigation if necessary. Monitoring of this kind is now commonplace on purpose-built high-speed lines, such as the TGV ones. The SNCF control centre at Frethun is the most complex and modern, with 850 routing activities; similarly the Signalling Centre at Ashford, built by Network SouthEast but now part of Railtrack, is of the most modern 'IECC' (Integrated Electronic Control Centre) type. The Eurotunnel control centres are built to the same technical standards, but are more complex because of the additional systems installed in the Tunnel.

Voice communication

Because the actions of individuals cannot be directly controlled by signals sent down a wire, voice links to and from the Control Centre are also provided. Five separate voice communication systems have been established. The first is a radio link between the trackside and the trains. This is supplemented by Eurotunnel's radio system which other operational staff

The road traffic controllers' view over the allocation lanes on the Calais Terminal

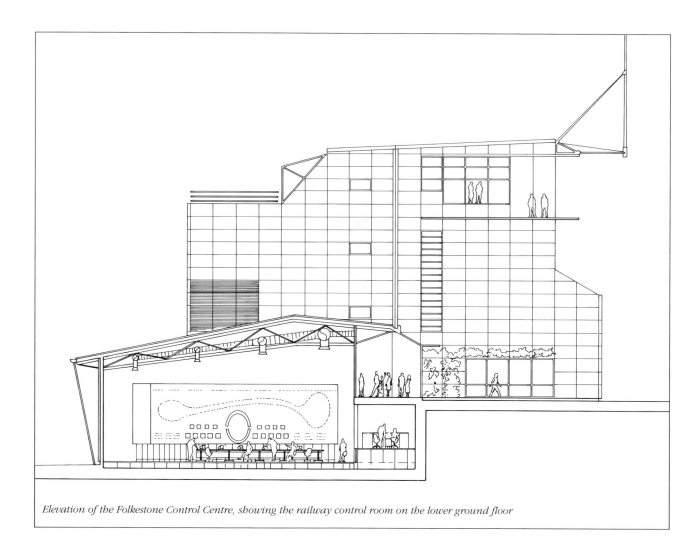

Elevation of the Folkestone Control Centre, showing the railway control room on the lower ground floor

use throughout the tunnels and the terminals. For normal communication purposes there is a telephone network in the terminals and tunnels, and special emergency phones are provided at appropriate points as on underground railway systems. Finally, a public address system enables the controllers to pass messages to staff throughout the terminal areas, as well as in the cross-passages and the service tunnel.

Major incident control

Should a particularly serious incident occur, requiring assistance from local emergency services, the Major Incident Co-ordination Centre would be established in one of the Incident Co-ordination Rooms as the focus for outside agencies to combine their resources and actions with those of Eurotunnel. This is equipped to give an overview of the state of operations, and provides conference facilities and access to the full communications network inside and outside Eurotunnel's area of responsibility. Numerous simulation exercises have been carried out, starting even before the Tunnel transportation system was complete, for which the consultants concerned, Black Mountain, received a national training award.

Appendix 1 – Electrical Traction Equipment

What is a GTO?

A GTO, or Gate Turn Off Thyristor, is an electronic switch which can be made to turn electric currents on and off hundreds of times a second. It is among the latest of the solid-state devices which have been developed since transistors started to replace the more complicated, bulky and fragile thermionic valves in radios, more than forty years ago. All these solid-state devices are manufactured from materials which are not metallic conductors like copper or iron, and are thus often referred to as 'semi-conductor' devices.

The simplest form of a solid-state device is a diode, which acts as a rectifier, allowing current to pass in one direction, and stopping it flowing in the other. This was followed by the transistor, which has a side contact added to it. By varying the voltage applied to this third terminal, the current through the device can be controlled. It is thus the solid-state equivalent of the thermionic triode. Current can still travel through the device in only one direction.

The solid-state thyristor is somewhat similar, and its 'gate' corresponds to the grid of a triode valve. However, although the grid in a valve can be used to turn the current 'off' as well as 'on', the gate of a thyristor can only switch the device 'on'. A thyristor is thus really the solid-state equivalent of the thyratron. To make such a device stop conducting it is necessary to reverse the overall polarity across it. When the voltage is again reversed, it needs a further pulse on the gate to make it start conducting again. The GTO thyristor is a much more highly-developed device, and, as its name implies, it can be switched off directly by applying a pulse of the opposite sign to the gate.

While transistors originally only passed extremely small currents and low voltages, thyristors and GTOs have now been developed that will deal with very large throughputs and 4500 volts, those on the shuttle locomotives being able to cope with more than 2500 amps.

General GTO thyristor scheme

Although the basic concept adopted for the shuttle locomotives relied heavily on other systems which had been built in Switzerland, the design details included some important innovations. For example, all the semi-conductor devices used in the traction section are GTO thyristors, an important innovation for a 6-motor main-line locomotive. Thanks to their specifications, only forty-five of these new-generation semi-conductors are necessary for a locomotive with a rating of 5.6MW at the wheels. In all, less than one hundred power semi-conductors, including diodes, are used to meet the total requirements for the traction and auxiliary power supplies. This is a third of the number needed in any previously comparable locomotive.

The electronic control is provided by programmable modules from the ASEA Brown Boveri (ABB) MICAS-S2 range, which reduces their volume by a factor of more than six compared with discrete control electronics. The MICAS traction-control electronics use new-generation microprocessors, of which there are six main units. This ensures that, even with a problem on one of the units, the locomotive will still be able to produce two-thirds of its full power output.

Transformers

Another important feature with the shuttle locomotives is the design of the transformer. The complex demands require equal impedances for the individual traction windings and the best possible insulation between them. Because the four-quadrant converter is optimised for maximum power transmission using the highest possible grid voltage and a sinusoidal converter voltage, this necessitates the individual transformer windings having a high leakage factor of 25 per cent. Most of the low-frequency harmonics are eliminated by staggered pulsing of the four-quadrant controllers. Any harmonics which do not occur lie in the range above 2000Hz, where the inherent characteristics of the equipment automatically attenuate them. In addition to the six traction windings, there are also separate transformer windings for the auxiliaries and, after rectification, to supply the 1500V dc train-line.

It can be seen from the main circuit diagram (see page 33) that there are pairs of parallel 'four-quadrant' power controllers for each bogie. (These are sometimes referred to as force-commutated single-phase bridges if they have an outside commutation circuit, as when used for 'choppers'.) After these there is the dc intermediate stage with a parallel resonant-filter circuit tuned to twice the main frequency, followed by a propulsion system with an inverter in two-pulse circuit, and parallel-connected star-wound motors.

Contactless voltage converter switching is possible for braking and motoring, as well as for reversing; the high grid reliability has removed the need for a rheostatic braking resistor. Synchronised alternate pulsing of the converters of the two bogies reduces the pulse amplitude at the transformer side, thus reducing interference in the grid. A high-voltage filter for reducing any harmonics is not therefore necessary. The interference current measured during normal operation is typically only 500mA.

Each of the four quadrant power converters generates a pulse-width modulated voltage with an R.M.S. value proportional to the transformer secondary voltage. The conversion frequency is continuously synchronised with the supply frequency, so that the phase angle between the supply voltage and the load current can be set to what is required. On these locomotives, during motoring an electric 'angle' of zero is used, and during braking this is changed to 180°. Because the voltage and current are kept in phase, and staggered pulsing reduces the harmonics, the total power factor is practically unity throughout the power range. This has been verified during tests, in the locomotive as well as on the 25kV side of the sub-stations, both under power and when braking.

Converters/Inverters

The 3-unit traction converters are oil-immersed – a design proved in almost twenty years' of service. The four-quadrant power controller and the propulsion system converter for each bogie are mounted in separate aluminium tanks; they are of identical design and fully interchangeable. These two main components of the converter system are linked with their oil-flow cooling circuits by flexible pipes which can be easily disconnected. The frame is a pre-assembled unit which also carries the capacitors of the voltage link and series resonant circuit, the main converters, and gate-control units, as well as the overall voltage limitation and protective gear, such as the earthing switch.

The converter's active section comprises individual phase modules, each with two GTOs and associated diodes, protection components and snubber circuitry.

The intermediate link voltage of 2800V requires semi-conductors with a blocking voltage of 4.5kV, while the current necessary to achieve the required power involves a turn off capability of at least 2500A.

The gate-control units of the GTO thyristors are mounted outside the tanks. They convert the optical-fibre signals arriving from the control electronics into the current pulses, which are then transmitted by coaxial cable to the semi-conductors. This ensures electromagnetic compatibility, as well as galvanic isolation between the main circuit and the control electronics.

Any instantaneous difference between the power being delivered by the GTOs and that required by the propulsion system is stored temporarily in capacitors in the dc link The propulsion system's inverter converts this into a three-phase variable output voltage with variable frequency. Depending upon the frequency range, either pulse-width modulation or the fundamental mode with three intermediate pulses is used. The maximum power output is reached at an output frequency of 23Hz, the maximum output voltage corresponding to a frequency of 130Hz. In these locomotives the full control capability of the drive converter is not used as it is the four-quadrant power controller in the propulsion chain that determines the overall power output.

Auxiliaries

The auxiliary equipment comprises fans for cooling the traction motors and the transformer/converter oil, the air-compressor, and oil pumps. The fan motors are fed by three-phase auxiliary converters which, like the traction converters, include GTOs. The use of a variable speed drive allows the ventilation to be started only when the oil temperature rises too high, instead of having to run continuously. Each bogie has its own auxiliary converter, referred to as the static auxiliary power supply. A parallel circuit supplies the power for the traction-motor fans, also at variable speed (35-55Hz), and the transformer oil-cooler. The power supply for the screw-type air compressor is a three-phase one, operating at a fixed frequency (50Hz) using separate converters.

The five 50kVA auxiliary power supply units are from ABB's BUR modular range. Their output inverters, which are also equipped with GTOs, are air-cooled modules capable of being supplied from different types of input converter. These inverters also vary the output voltage; their mode of operation is similar to that of the traction converters, although at a considerably lower power level. The input converters used on these locomotives are asymmetric rectifiers, and line-commutated, which is adequate for the low power level used.

Appendix 2 – Temporary locomotives: SNCF Class 22200/22400

When the delivery schedule of the shuttle locomotives and the Class 92 locomotives (see chapter 7) became delayed, Eurotunnel, BR and SNCF considered using existing locomotives for certain operations through the Tunnel between the Folkestone Terminal or Dollands Moor and the north of France. SNCF's Class 22200 ac/dc locomotive was selected. Some 202 were built between 1976 and 1986, originally for use on the line between Paris, Rennes and Nantes; they now appear widely on French main lines. The continental loading gauge limits their operation in Britain to the Dollands Moor freight marshalling area, just outside the Folkestone Terminal. Nine Class 22200 locomotives were modified to operate in the Tunnel, six with TVM 430 and three without. The former are numbered 22379/80/99/22401/3/5, and have the letters TTU on their noses and sides; those without TVM 430 are 22400/2/4, and have the initials TU.

General features

Class 22200 locomotives are dual voltage, 25kV ac and 1500V dc, rated at 3780kW and weighing 90 tonnes. They are a development of the dc Class 7200 locomotives, which give the same power output and weigh 84 tonnes. All the Class 22200s are of B-B configuration with four driving axles and only two traction motors. In northern France and in the Channel Tunnel, they will work only on 25kV lines. From this supply a 25,000/1500V transformer feeds a mixed thyristor and diode bridge, which in turn feeds six constant-voltage dc/variable voltage (0 to 1600V) dc choppers with thyristors and auxiliaries. Three of these choppers in parallel control the dc current for one motor. Thus a total of twenty diodes and forty thyristors is needed on the ac side and forty thyristors on the dc side, a total power component of 188 semi-conductors. The continuous rating of the traction motors is in the range 3780kW at 58km/h to 4300kW at 103km/h, with a maximum speed of 160km/h. The locomotives are equipped with electro-pneumatic braking, a driver's safety device handle, constant speed control and an anti-wheelslip device.

Class 22400 in the Channel Tunnel

The locomotives can be employed to haul freight through-trains and sleeper trains (see chapter 7) as well as Eurotunnel's test freight shuttles. Although only a single locomotive is required to haul the freight through-trains, a second may be needed to provide sufficient power for heavily loaded trains. Two locomotives are required for the night services and four for the freight shuttles, divided equally between each end of the train so that it can be split or reversed.

Freight through-trains weighing more than 900 tonnes will generally be operated by two Class 22400s, with separate drivers, at the front of the train. The modifications required for this include: pantograph control from the front locomotive; control of high-speed circuit-breakers from the front locomotive; telephone link between the two driver's cabs; electric feed to the auxiliary signal panel in the rear locomotive; and interconnection of constant-speed control device. The front locomotive must be equipped with TVM 430 (see chapter 11), with an illuminated speed panel in each driver's cab. The second locomotive need not be equipped with TVM 430 so long as it remains permanently coupled. The driver is required in the

Two of the 22400 locomotives at the UK portal

second locomotive to control the traction power, working to the overall command of the driver on the first locomotive.

Modifications

The modifications required to enable Class 22400s to run through the Tunnel were carried out by Oullins Machines at SNCF's workshops near Lyon. The principal changes are described below.

Driver's cab

1 New ventilation and heating equipment, as well as a small fan on the driver's desk, was installed. As on the shuttle locomotives, this equipment can operate for 90 minutes without power from the catenary.

2 Doors, windows, and windscreen washers were resealed to increase fire resistance and reduce noise inside the cab.

3 Auxiliary lighting for dual-locomotive operation and other controls was installed on the driver's desk.

Electrical equipment

Circuit modifiers were required to cut the supply to the two low-voltage stabilisers for the electronics, which have a high power consumption, in the event of the catenary supply failing. With this modification, the original battery design provides sufficient power for

ninety minutes without catenary supply.

Fire protection

Fire-detection and -extinguishing equipment was installed in the central cubicle near the main power electronics, one set near the battery and one in the high-speed breaker cubicle. In addition, a duplicate automatic fire-detection system and Halon gas extinguishers were fitted.

Other modifications

Improvements were incorporated in the safety-valves on the transformer cooling system. Tests were carried out to ensure that harmonics or electromagnetic interference induced by the presence of the third rail at Dollands Moor does not affect the locomotives' safety or operation.

To conform to British safety requirements, the locomotives have been given yellow noses to make them more visible to people working on the track.

Appendix 3 – Standard-gauge construction motive power

During the main Tunnel construction period, all materials, equipment and personnel were transported to and from the tunnel boring machines and other work areas on rolling stock using the 900mm-gauge construction railway. This gauge was selected to enable

The unusual design of one of the X3800 'Picasso' diesel railcars can be seen from this photograph taken in the middle of the Tunnel during the first crossing from France to England

The former Belgian Railways' three-car diesel-hydraulic railcar No. 4001, hired by TML from Chemin de Fer des Trois Vallées

Former BR three-car diesel-mechanical railcar in the Tunnel. This set was used by Regional Railways, being based at Tyseley, on the outskirts of Birmingham. It was used for suburban services, the design dating from 1959

One of the former BR Class 20 Bo-Bo diesel-electric locomotives hired by TML from RFS Engineering at the French portal. The large-diameter pipe across the cab took the exhaust gases to the scrubber on the first wagon

two tracks to be laid in each tunnel, including the narrower service tunnel. The construction railway was a complex and heavily used rail system in its own right.

During the later construction stages of the tunnels and terminals, many of the contractors and sub-contractors employed a variety of standard-gauge locomotives for different purposes. The most intensive use was in the course of building the walkways and laying the standard-gauge track in the rail tunnels, when trains 580m long, weighing up to 2000 tonnes, were needed to convey the quantities of concrete required. All the rails and the blocks supporting them were also taken in by standard-gauge train, and special gantries were used to lift them off and move them forward, to be laid on the first-stage concrete in the base of the tunnels.

Two classes of diesel locomotive were used for this work, the majority being former BR Class 20 Bo-Bo diesel-electrics of 746kW, built by English-Electric from 1957 onwards. More than a dozen of these were hired from RFS Engineering of Doncaster, who had refurbished them after purchasing them from BR or hiring them from preservation societies. These operated from both terminals, but some former Deutsches Bundesbahn Class 211 B-B diesel-hydraulics of 820kW were also used by the Channel Tunnel Trackwork Group at Folkestone. In addition RFS provided one of the former BR Class 08 0-6-0 diesel-electric shunters of 298kW, which was also painted in their own livery.

After the laying of the final track in the tunnels was complete, TML used standard-gauge diesel railcars to transport staff to their work-places, instead of relying on the slower construction-gauge manriders in the service tunnel. At the French end, five former SNCF Series X3800 diesel railcars were hired from Compagnie de Chemins de Fer et Transport Auxiliaires. These had operated on different private railways, and were refurbished by Société Auxiliaire de Diesels (SAD) at Florange, near Thionville. From 1950 onwards, some 250 of these single-car units were constructed for SNCF by various builders, being known as 'Picassos' because of their unusual appearance. (Some are still used in the

A former DBB B-B diesel-hydraulic locomotive No. 211 134-2 in the Folkestone Terminal. This was one of the class purchased by CTTG, and given its number 22

summer on tourist lines.) A three-car Belgian railcar with hydraulic transmission was also hired from Chemin de Fer des Trois Vallées.

At the UK end, three former BR three-car diesel-mechanical railcars were hired for the same purpose. They

One of the former BR 0-6-0 Class 08 diesel-electric shunters in the Folkestone Terminal. Several hundred of this general design were built from 1963 onwards, this one being purchased by RFS Engineering, and leased to TML. The owner's fleet of 08s were all given names ending in -ence, this being Florence. A similar locomotive, still in BR service, can be seen in the photograph on page 34

dated from the late 1950s, when many such sets were constructed as part of the 1955 Modernisation Plan, and by the 1990s were being replaced by more modern stock.

As the railcars were limited to a maximum of 30km/h, like the other trains using the Tunnel before the signalling was installed, their gear-box controls were modified to ensure that they could not exceed this speed.

Appropriate exhaust treatment equipment was provided for these locomotives and railcars to meet the environmental requirements in the Tunnel.

Appendix 4 – Maintenance and works trains

A variety of rolling stock is required for maintenance and works trains (see also chapter 5). To achieve greatest flexibility and provide for a range of different activities, these have been designed as modules capable of being mounted on flat-wagons. This produces a cost-effective and flexible means of having over thirty modules available, of which, however, only fifteen are required to be in use at any one time. Catenary, track, cleaning, mechanical, signalling and communications maintenance trains can thus be made up using one common type of wagon.

Fifteen flat-wagons were supplied by SOCOFER, near Tours, to accommodate the modules. Three Bulgarian wagons had already been purchased and were used in the initial stages of commissioning.

Amenity module

Basket crane for overhead working

Specialised crane for pipework

Cleaning-out tanks

Gauge measurement

Fixed gantry for Tunnel maintenance

The following modules were supplied:

Quantity	Description	Length (metres)
2	Elevator gantry for catenary maintenance	9
1	Basket crane for overhead working	9
1	Coil support for 3.05m diameter spool	6
2	Coil support for 1.5m diameter spool	6, 9
3	Amenity module	9
4	Specialised crane for pipework	6, 9
2	Gantry for rails and track	6, 9
1	Crane for piston relief duct valves	9
2	Cleaning-out tanks	12
1	Gauge measurement	6
2	Fixed gantry	6, 9
2	Tunnel-cleaning equipment	6, 9
3	Flat with slatted sides	6, 9
6	Flat	6, 9

Elevator gantry for catenary maintenance and, right, for rail maintenance

Appendix 5 – Eurostar Trains

Principal details

The following are the principal details of the '2 + 18' Eurostar sets, series 373, numbered from 3001 on the locomotive.

Overall length	394m (20 vehicles)
Maximum width	2.8m
Weight in working order	752 tonnes
Weight laden	816 tonnes
Maximum axle load	17 tonnes
Driving configuration	Each of the two axles on the bogies of the power cars is driven by its own asynchronous traction motor, as is the outer bogie of the next vehicle to it. There are thus 12 motorised bogies on each train.

Maximum speed in service 300km/h

Continuous ratings

at 25kV ac	12.2MW (16,350hp)
at 3kV dc	5.7MW (7640hp)
at 750V dc (nominal)	3.4MW (4560hp)

Seating capacity (18 vehicles)

1st class	210
2nd class	584 + 52 folding seats

Formation of standard Eurostar trains

The trains consist of two half-sets, symmetrical about their centres. There is a separate power-car at each end, and the remaining vehicles in the half-set are articulated together. For operational purposes, the passenger-carrying vehicles are numbered R1 to R18.

Coach numbers	Vehicle use
R1/R18	One power bogie, with equipment compartment: nursery area: 52 2nd-class seats (non-smoking)
R2/R17	60 2nd-class seats (non-smoking)
R3/R16	60 2nd-class seats (non-smoking)
R4/R15	60 2nd-class seats (smoking)
R5/R14	60 2nd-class seats (smoking)
R6/R13	Buffet bar: 2 catering stores
R7/R12	Lounge area: 39 1st-class seats (smoking)
R8/R11	Lounge area: 39 1st-class seats (non-smoking)
R9/R10	Baggage compartment: 2 customs compartments: space and WC for disabled passengers: 29 1st-class seats (non-smoking)

The 'North of England' sets have four fewer trailers, giving a '2 + 14' formation, which reduces their length to 340m. They have 114 first-class seats and 464 2nd-class. Compared with the standard sets, additional accommodation has been provided in cars R9/10 for border control staff, which enables the British customs and passport checks to be carried out on board.

The power equipment of the Eurostar trains, supplied by GEC Alsthom, is similar to that of the Eurotunnel and Class 92 locomotives, particularly in respect of three-phase variable-frequency traction-motors. The only difference involves the single-phase rectification from 25kV ac, which is carried out using a transformer provided with a silicon-oil cooling system, together with a 'bridge' comprising GTOs and thyristors. In the Tunnel the system operates at reduced power and temperature levels, where the train runs at a maximum of 160km/h. When the trains are running on the 3kV and 750V dc systems, 'choppers' are used to reduce or increase the voltage in the intermediate dc circuits feeding the traction-motor inverters.

Acknowledgements

The authors and publisher would like to thank all the many people who have contributed to the research and production for this book, in particular: Tony Berkeley, John Chapman, Tom Farling, Alan Goldfinch (former BR Electrification Engineer), David Hart, Colin Kirkland, Dominique Lartrilleux, Graeme Overall, Wendy Quick, Pauline Robertson, Josef Scheerens, Richard Storer and Jeremy Wilson.

Project managers:	Tony Berkeley and Claire Whiddon
Designer:	Julie Cooke
Editor and publishing consultant:	Christopher Pick
Illustration research:	Julie Cooke, Peter Semmens and Yves Machefert-Tassin
Photographic research:	Colin Stephens
Index:	Indexing Specialists, Hove
Production:	Monica Kochhar

Illustrations by TDA, London except:

Transmanche-Link/Kalligraphic Design 62, 99 (top left and right); Lee Tucker 8, 13, 14, 44, 46 (top), 53 (top), 57, 67, 77, 87, 98, 112

Reproduction: Swift Graphics (UK) Limited

Photography by QA Photos Ltd, except:

ASEA Brown Boveri 32; Philippe Demail 18, 60; European Passenger Services Ltd 104; Mike Griggs 138; Yves Machefert-Tassin 28 (left), 29, 30, 32 (bottom right), 51 (bottom), 65 (centre), 71, 89, 92, 135 (right), 136, 151 (top left and bottom left), 153; Milepost 92, 109 (left); Nederlandse Spoorwegen 88 (left); Phot'R 6, 119; Railfreight Distribution 108, 109 (right); R. C. Riley 152 (left); Peter Semmens 59 (right); Transmanche-Link 16, 68, 74 (right)

The photographs reproduced in this book were taken during the construction and commissioning phases of the project. A few are of variable quality, or show unfinished works; these have been included to illustrate aspects of the system that could not otherwise have been shown.

Further Reading

Railway magazines provide virtually the only significant source of further reading on Channel Tunnel trains. In the UK, *The Railway Magazine* (IPC Magazines) has carried a monthly article by Peter Semmens since January 1990, and also published a supplement, 'Channel Tunnel Update' with the October 1989 edition, while *Rail* (EMAP) also carries regular Channel Tunnel news. *Railway Gazette International* (Reed Business Publishing – by subscription only) and *Modern Railways* (Ian Allan) have both carried frequent articles. A special Channel Tunnel supplement is being included in the May 1994 issue of *Railway Gazette International*. The bilingual *Eurotunnel News*, published by Eurotunnel, is a further useful source of information.

In France, *Revue Générale des Chemins de Fer* (Dunod) is an important source, and also published Transmanche special issues in December 1993 and February 1994. *Chemins de Fer* (A.F.A.C.) also carries regular features; see especially the March 1990, June 1991 and February and March 1994 issues. The coverage in *La Vie du Rail* is also thorough; see especially the edition of 2 May 1991.

Train Technology for the Tunnel (Proceedings of the Institution of Mechanical Engineers, no. 8, 1992) contains papers presented at an international conference held at Le Touquet in November 1992. The proceedings of an earlier seminar, held in London in April 1990, on Channel

Tunnel Rolling Stock were published by the Institution's Railway Division.

The proceedings of the 26th Conference on Modern Rail Vehicles held at Graz Technical University, Austria, in October 1990 were published as 'Der Tunnel durch den Ärmelkanal' in *Verkehrsannalen, ZEV-DET, Die Eisenbahn Technik* (Georg Siemens Verlagsbuchhandlung, Berlin, 1991).

In contrast, the more general literature on the history, construction and financing of the Channel Tunnel is vast. Space precludes the mention of more than a few titles here. Jeremy Wilson and Jérome Spick, *Eurotunnel: the Illustrated Journey* (HarperCollins, 1994) is the official illustrated account of construction. Derek Wilson, *Breakthrough* (Century, 1991) relates the story of construction up to the breakthrough of the service tunnel in December 1990. Bertrand Lemoine, *Le Tunnel sous la Manche* (Editions du Moniteur, 1991) surveys the history of the Tunnel and construction progress to the date of publication. Two volumes of the Proceedings of The Institution of Civil Engineers - Part 1: *Tunnels* (1992) and Part 2: *Terminals* (1993) - provide a technical account of UK construction by engineers closely involved. Colin Kirkland (editor), *Engineering the Channel Tunnel* (James & James, forthcoming, 1994) is a detailed survey of the problems faced by the Tunnel's

engineers and of solutions reached. Michael R Bonavia, *The Channel Tunnel Story* (David & Charles, 1987) describes the various Channel Tunnel schemes, leading to the formation of Eurotunnel. Peter Semmens, *Channel Tunnel: Engineering Triumph of the Century* (a *Railway Magazine* special for IPC Magazines, 1994) is a description of the Tunnel and all the related railway activities. Mitchell P Strohl, *Europe's High-Speed Trains: a study in geo-economics* (Praeger, 1993) fills in the economic and commercial background to the development of a high-speed European rail network, and includes a chapter on the troubled high-speed link from the Tunnel to London. Paul Varley, *From Charing Cross to Baghdad* (Eurotunnel, 1992) surveys early attempts to build the Channel Tunnel, and focuses on the hitherto little-known scheme in the early 1920s.

Eurotunnel's own publications on the current project include the three issues of *Progress in Pictures* (1990, 1991 and 1993), which provide a photographic account of construction; *Committed to Safety* (1994), a detailed account of the safety measures built into the construction and operation of the Tunnel; and *La Construction du tunnel sous la Manche* (1993), which focuses largely on construction on the French side.

All the books mentioned above are available from good bookshops. For Eurotunnel publications, and in

case of difficulty, contact Mail Order Department, Eurotunnel Exhibition Centre, Cheriton High Street, Folkestone, Kent CT19 4QD (tel: 0303-273300). Eurotunnel also publishes a comprehensive range of illustrated booklets and technical papers on many aspects of the history, construction and environment of the Channel Tunnel; for details, contact the Mail Order Department.